What is Truth?

C. J. F. Will.

Reader in Philosophy, University of Bristol

Cambridge University Press

Cambridge

London . New York . Melbourne

Published by the Syndics of the Cambridge University Press
The Pitt Building, Trumpington Street, Cambridge CB2 1RP
Bentley House, 200 Euston Road, London, NW1 2DB
32 East 57th Street, New York, NY 10022, USA
296 Beaconsfield Parade, Middle Park, Melbourne 3206, Australia

First published 1976

Printed in Great Britain
at the
University Printing House, Cambridge
(Euan Phillips, University Printer)

Library of Congress Cataloguing in Publication Data
Williams, Christopher John Fards
   What is truth?
   Bibliography: p. 99
   Includes index
   1.   Truth. I. Title
BD171.W53   111.8'3   75–23533
ISBN 0 521 20967 6

Ἔχειν αὐτὸ δεῖ οὕτως ὡς λέγομεν·
εἰ γὰρ μὴ οὕτως ἔχει, οὐκ ἂν ἀληθῆ
λέγοιμεν.
(PLATO, *Parmenides*, 161 e 4–5)

*Denn, wahr ist ein Satz, wenn es sich so
verhält, wie wir es durch ihn sagen.*
(WITTGENSTEIN, *Tractatus*, 4.062)

Contents

Preface

Despite a perfect ignorance of the works of Hegel, I should hazard the claim that this book is not remotely Hegelian. It may, nevertheless, properly be described as 'dialectical'. It has written itself by way of advancing a series of positions each of which involves abandoning to some extent the position previously held. The later positions, however, build on the earlier. They would not be readily intelligible to persons who had not first grappled with the earlier positions. The earlier positions are also more simply statable than the later, and it is an advantage to be able to state simply at an early stage a doctrine which is at least a crude version of the doctrine finally arrived at. The later versions of the doctrine are refinements of this crude version. In the interests of accuracy these refinements have to be made. The interests of plausibility may also be served by the refinements, because objections that suggest themselves against the crude version are, it is hoped, replied to in the refining process. But plausibility is also achieved by a short, sharp, easily understood thesis, as that 'What Percy says is true' means no more than 'For some p, both Percy says that p and p'. Falsehood as well as truth may of course be made to look plausible; but if the first version of the thesis is not the whole truth about truth it is still, I believe, a good deal more true than false. It is not indeed until we have discussed falsehood that the whole truth can emerge. Perhaps even then it is rash, as well as brash, to claim to have told the whole truth about truth. From then on at least, I of course maintain, the story I tell if not the whole truth contains nothing but the truth.

Chapter 1 begins by stating the short, sharp thesis, but it turns almost immediately to difficulties which have been found in the practice of binding sentential variables with a quantifier and, more specifically, in placing them in an 'opaque' context like 'Percy says that'. It contends that the alleged contrast between 'substitutional' and 'objectual' quantification turns on a characterization of the latter which treats existence as a first-order predicate. Chapter 2 investigates the possibility of regarding truth as such a predicate. Two theories which would dispense with truth as a predicate are shown to fail, and a distinction drawn between the predicates to be discovered in 'As A's statement states, X is eligible' and in 'Things are as A's statement states'. The latter may be said to embody a predicate equivalent to '— is true' and expressible as 'For some p, both — states that p and p'. Chapter 3 examines expressions which could fill the gap in this last expression. Such expressions, it finds, are typically analogous to definite descriptions, expressions representable as having the form 'The p such that both Percy says nothing except that p and ( ) p'. Like definite descriptions they are incomplete symbols and do not name anything, so the question whether they name Propositions[1] or judgements or beliefs does not arise. But, whereas 'Louis XV is sole king of France and is bald', the truth of which would make 'The King of France is bald' true, mentions Louis XV, 'Percy says that Mabel has measles and Percy says nothing else and Mabel *has* measles', the truth of which would make 'What Percy says is true' true, mentions nothing except Percy and Mabel. The analysis given in this chapter of 'What Percy says is true' is an advance on that given in Chapter 1 because it allows for the uniqueness of what Percy says; and it is an advance on that given in Chapter 2 because the apparent predicate 'is true' disappears from the analysis without leaving behind any expression simply substitutable for it. Chapter 4 takes the analysis a step further. On the account given in Chapter 3 'What Percy says is true' and 'What Percy says is false' would be contraries, not contradictories. Both would entail 'Percy says just one thing'. It is now argued that they presuppose rather than entail this, and that each asserts two propositions rather than one: 'Percy says just one thing' is asserted by each of them, but the other proposition asserted by 'What Percy says is true' is indeed the contradictory of the other proposition asserted by 'What Percy says is false'. Chapter 5, the

[1] For an explanation of the way in which the term 'proposition' is used in this book see Geach (3), §19. Following Geach I shall 'dignify "Proposition" with an initial capital' when it purports to refer to a non-linguistic entity.

last chapter, does not claim to take the analysis further but only to examine its relationship to the Correspondence Theory of Truth. It is argued that, so far from the notion of correspondence being needed in order to make sense of the analysis here provided, the analysis itself gives an account of the notion of correspondence along with that of truth. The notion of correspondence may be thought to give expression to the feeling that truth is in some way relational. The extent to which such a feeling is justified is here determined.

The doctrines for which I argue are, to a large extent, inherited from the discoveries made in Philosophical Logic by the late Arthur Prior. I should like to think of them as carrying further work which he had already begun. Indeed it seems to me that all the major obstacles to progress in this field had been removed by him before I began to work in it. The other main teacher to whom I owe insights put to use in this book is Professor P. T. Geach. My thinking on the subject began by my being moved to dispute some of the points made by 'In Disputation of an Undisputed Thesis' by Dr O. R. Jones, which appeared in *Analysis* in 1968 (vol. 28, no. 4). Further articles by Dr Jones in the same journal resisted points made by my 'What does "x is true" say about x?' (*Analysis*, vol. 29, no. 4, 1969) and our controversy spilled over from the pages of *Analysis* into a private correspondence. I learned much from these discussions. Some of what I say in these pages repeats what I said in my *Analysis* articles ('Truth: a composite rejoinder' in vol. 32, no. 2, 1971, as well as the one already mentioned), in 'Truth: or Bristol Revisited' (*Proceedings of the Aristotelian Society*, supplementary volume XLVII, 1973), in 'Prior and Ontology' (*Ratio*, vol. 15, 1973) and in 'Predicating Truth' (*Mind*, vol. 84, 1975). I am grateful to the editors of these journals for permission to incorporate some of the material already published.

Where I have used symbols for logical constants I have used Polish notation. For those not familiar with this I list here the Russellian equivalents of the Polish symbols I have used: $Np = \sim p$; $Kpq = p \cdot q$; $Apq = p \vee q$; $Cpq = p \supset q$; $Epq = p \equiv q$; $\Sigma xFx = (\exists x)Fx$; $\Pi xFx = (x)Fx$; $Ixy = x = y$. The advantage is of course that brackets are unnecessary in this notation.

At some points in the text there may seem to be an undue proliferation of logical symbolism. My aim has been to use it only when its use avoids tedious repetition and the more long-winded sentences that would be the result of adhering religiously to 'ordinary language'. A word should be said, however, to forestall those who are reluctant to believe that formal logic can provide much aid in exposing the structure of ordinary language. The logical symbols on which I have most chiefly relied are quantifiers. A piece of jargon introduced by Prior can, I think, do a good deal to help our understanding of quantifiers. An existential proposition like 'Someone is coming to dinner' is true if a corresponding singular proposition like 'Michael is coming to dinner' is true. Prior called propositions of the latter sort 'verifiers' of propositions of the former sort. It is arguable that an existential proposition is understood if, and only if, we understand what sort of proposition would count as a verifier of it. Somewhat simplified, the thesis of this book is that propositions like 'Percy says that Mabel has measles and Mabel has measles' stand to propositions like 'What Percy says is true' in the same relation as 'Michael is coming to dinner' stands to 'Someone is coming to dinner'. In each case the former proposition is a verifier of the latter. All four propositions are, of course, expressed in 'ordinary' English and the logical relation of verifier to proposition verified holds between them as so expressed. 'What Percy says is true' is understood, I should maintain, if, and only if, we understand that a proposition like 'Percy says that Mabel has measles and Mable has measles' would count as a verifier of it. The symbolic analogue of 'Someone is coming to dinner', 'For some x, x is coming to dinner', serves the purpose of showing more clearly what sort of proposition would count as a verifier in this case – namely, a true proposition obtained by dropping 'For some x,' and substituting a name for 'x' in its second occurrence. Similarly, the symbolic analogue of 'What Percy says is true', 'For some p, both Percy says that p and p', serves the purpose of showing more clearly what sort of proposition would count as a verifier in *this* case – namely, a true proposition obtained by dropping 'For some p,' and substituting a sentence for 'p' in its second and third occurrences. Part of the use of the quantifier and the variables is to provide, as it were, a *demonstratio ad oculos* of the relation between verifier and proposition verified. The relation is there – in 'ordinary language' – without benefit of symbols. No one who understands the words can fail to agree that if Percy says that Mabel has measles and Mabel *has* measles what Percy says is true. The invention of the (modest) symbolism involved in 'For some p, both Percy says that p and p' is valuable amongst other things for its exposing an underlying structure that was there all the time.

On the other side, the suggestion that the meaning of 'What Percy says is true' is given, roughly, by 'For some p, both Percy says that p and p', once made, will seem to some so obvious that it is difficult for them to imagine how a whole book, albeit a short one, could justifiably be devoted to the subject. To them it may be replied, first, that the analysis so far given is indeed a rough one and the attempt to make it more precise involves a good deal of labour. The second part of my reply concedes much of the point of their objection. Like Ramsey's so-called 'Redundancy Theory', of which it may be regarded as a development, mine is a theory which aims at making many of the traditional problems about Truth disappear. Truth, as one of Mackie's titles suggests,[1] is more simple than has been thought. But philosophers often have to work quite hard merely to undo the damage that has been caused by their predecessors. Obstacles raised to the use of simple devices such as propositional quantification have to be removed. Objections to the possibility of giving a general answer to the question 'What is it that "x is true" says about x?' have to be answered. Most importantly, perhaps, puzzles about what sort of things, if any, can be called 'true', can be the bearers of truth, have to be solved. 'What is truth?' cannot be answered without an answer being given to the allied question 'What are truths?' Our answer to this question, involving as it does the clarification of such matters as the nature of Propositions and definite descriptions, may be thought to produce a pay-off outside the strict limits of a theory of truth.

A draft of the book was read in whole or in part by several friends, and I have been much assisted by their comments and criticisms. I wish to record my gratitude for this to J. L. Mackie, A. R. White,

[1] Cf. Mackie (1).

O. R. Jones, Keith Graham and P. T. Geach. The book had already been accepted for publication before I came across the article by Dorothy L. Grover *et al.* 'A Prosentential Theory of Truth'. I am aware that a good deal of what I say is anticipated by these authors, though I believe there is enough difference between us to leave room for the book. If I had had more time to digest their article I should have wished to make explicit connections between points they make and points I make at numerous places in the text. I look forward to their reaction to what I have written.

This book is dedicated to the memory of my father, Harold William Fardo Williams, who died while it was being written.

C.J.F.W.

Midsomer Norton
Holy Week, mcmlxxv

I

How simple is truth?

What sort of a thing is truth, and what sort of things are truths? Philosophers have found these questions very perplexing. *Truth* has been called a transcendental attribute, being placed thereby in the same category as being and goodness – or rather these attributes have been said to be alike in that they transcend all categories. *Truths* have been identified with the most various entities: with concrete physical entities such as particular inscriptions, with concrete mental entities such as particular thoughts or ideas; with abstract entities such as types or classes of mental or physical entities of the kinds mentioned; and with abstract entities other than classes related by the mysterious relation 'expressed by' to these physical or mental entities, abstractions which have been called 'Propositions'[1] or 'Sätze an sich'.

And yet the answer is so simple. To say that what Percy says is true is to say that things are as Percy says they are, i.e. (at least as a rough approximation) that

(1)   For some p, both Percy says that p and p.

In order to understand what is meant by calling what someone says true, we have only to understand what is meant by someone's saying something, by 'some' and by 'and'. The difficulty lies in seeing the connections between such apparently object-designating expressions as 'What Percy says' and such an apparently predicative expression as 'is true' and (1). If such connections are not traced, the problems seem to be, what objects do expressions like 'What Percy says' designate, and what property does the predicative expression 'is true' ascribe.

Some philosophers do not agree that (1) is as simple as all that. It is not, after all, *quite* ordinary English. This first chapter is devoted to explaining what is meant by (1), and attempting to meet

---

[1]   *Vide supra*, p. xii, note.

some objections that are likely to be made to its employment.

How are we to understand (1)? It contains a variable-letter, '*p*', three times repeated. Elementary algebra familiarizes us with the notion of a variable: '$x^2+2x-24 = 0$' told us that some number was such that subtracting 24 from the sum of its square and its double would leave us with nothing. If we could find out what number it was, substituting the corresponding numeral for '*x*' in the equation would yield a true arithmetical proposition

$$(4^2+2.4-24 = 0).$$

Understanding this use of '*x*' was a matter of understanding the relation of '*x*' to the numerals whose substitution for it was capable of producing true or false arithmetical propositions.

Similarly, to understand (1) we must understand a relation between '*p*' and a certain class of expressions. By convention the variable-letters '*p*', '*q*', '*r*', etc., are connected in logic to sentences in a way similar to that in which '*x*', '*y*' and '*z*' are connected in algebra to numerals. We begin to understand (1) if we realize that by removing 'For some *p*,' and substituting a complete sentence for each occurrence of '*p*' in what follows – the same sentence for each occurrence of it – we can produce a true or false proposition. Thus 'Percy says that Mabel has measles and Mabel has measles' itself says something either true or false. If what it says is true, (1) is true, and what Percy says is true, and 'What Percy says is true' is true.

These things would be true too if Percy said that Philip was dead and Philip was dead, or if Percy said that mice eat cheese and mice do eat cheese. The last example shows us that we need not be pernickety about what counts as repetition of the same sentence. It clearly makes no difference whether we replace '*p*' in both its occurrences after the 'both' in (1) by 'Mice eat cheese' or whether we replace it by 'Mice eat cheese' in its first occurrence and 'Mice do eat cheese' in its second occurrence. Sometimes repetition of exactly the same words is idiomatically impossible or clumsy in English. If what Percy said was that Charles would grow out of his shyness, then what Percy said was true if either Percy said that Charles would grow out of his shyness and Charles has grown out of his shyness, or Percy said that Charles would grow out of his shyness and Charles will grow out of his shyness. English idiom does not allow us to say 'Percy said that Charles would grow out of his shyness and Charles would grow out of his shyness'.

2

The type of analysis of truth we are offering is due in great measure to the methods employed in this area by the late Arthur Prior. Prior has been criticized by L. J. Cohen[1] precisely on the grounds that these features of English idiom block a mechanical reading of some of his formulae. For instance. 'For every p, if both Percy says that p and, for every q, if Percy says that q, q, then p' would according to Prior's usage express a logical truth. There is no difficulty in recognizing the following substitution instance of it as true: 'If both Percy says that it is raining and, for every q, if Percy says that q, q, then it is raining'. But the similarly produced instance 'If both Percy said that I should be met at the station and, for every q, if Percy says that q, q, then I should be met at the station' is false. It is false because 'I should be met at the station' has a sense as an independent sentence, equivalent, roughly, to 'I ought to be met at the station'. In its first occurrence, however, it represents a modification of 'I shall be met at the station' when this sentence is subordinated to a past-tense verb like 'said'. The example we gave above, where the subordinate sentence is 'Charles would grow out of his shyness' produces not falsehood but unidiomatic English, because this sentence has no plausible use other than its use in a subordinate clause after a past-tense verb.

It would not be difficult to standardize our sentences – put them into 'logical form', so to speak – so as to make these difficulties disappear. Thus, if we use a tense-operator like 'It was the case that' as a prefix to our past-tense sentences we can convert the sentence about Charles and his shyness into idiomatic, if clumsy, English: 'It was the case that both Percy said that Charles would grow out of his shyness and Charles would grow out of his shyness'. Again, if we take into account not only what it is appropriate for us to say now, given the truth of 'What Percy said is true', but what it would have been appropriate to say at an earlier time, we

---

[1] Cohen (1).

can find a sentence which allows mechanical substitution for the
sentential variable '*p*'. If someone had said at the time of Percy's
utterance 'Percy says that Charles will grow out of his shyness and
Charles will grow out of his shyness' the truth of what this person
said will guarantee the truth of 'What Percy said is true'. These
adjustments of tense etc. in the light of what different people might
appropriately say at different times are part of what every English
speaker knows in virtue of his ability to use tensed verbs in English.
This ability is involved in the ability to detect when a statement
like 'What Percy said is true' is justified, and the knowledge that
is here presupposed *is* the knowledge required to recognize substitutions for '*p*' in (1) as appropriate. Transformational grammarians
may have interesting things to say in the course of making such
knowledge explicit. But logicians need not wait for their results.
They are as much entitled to take 'Percy said that Charles would
grow out of his shyness and Charles has grown out of his shyness'
as a substitution instance of 'Percy said that *p* and *p*' as they are to
take 'She thought that Barbara ought to pay her' as a substitution
instance of '*x* thought that Barbara ought to pay *x*' without bog-
gling at the change of case from 'she' to 'her'.

3

The difficulties philosophers have made about the interpretation of
such formulae as (1) vary in importance. I am adopting the tactic
of dealing with them in increasing order of importance – or, where
the last and the next difficulties are concerned, in decreasing order of
unimportance.

Philosophers in the grip of a well-known theory[1] will object that
(1) involves 'quantification into an opaque context' and is therefore
illegitimate. 'Percy says that...' is an opaque context. What this
means is shortly to be explained. 'For some *p*,' in (1) is or includes
a quantifier. 'Quantification *into* an opaque context' is sometimes
taken in a mechanistic way as describing what we get when a
quantifier which appears in a sentence to the left of some words

---

[1] I refer, of course, to W. V. Quine's views about 'referential opacity'
expressed notably in 'Reference and Modality' in Quine (2) and in §§ 30, 35
of Quine (3).

which constitute an opaque context, i.e. outside that context, binds variables occurring to the right of those words in the same sentence, i.e. inside the opaque context. Certainly in (1) the phrase 'For some p,' appears to the left of the words 'Percy says that. . .' and binds variables which appear to the right of these words. But a more sensitive account is needed of what it is to be 'inside' or 'outside' an opaque context, and this cannot be given without examining the notion of 'opacity' itself.

Accounts of opacity are usually introduced by means of the prior notion of *purely referential position*. A purely referential position is one in which different expressions referring to the same object can be substituted for each other *salva veritate*. If 'Percy says that. . .' is taken as an opaque context this is because certain positions in what follows it, e.g. the position marked by 'x' in 'Percy says that x is a fast driver', are not regarded as purely referential. What is forbidden is for a quantifier outside the context to bind a variable in such a position. The discussion is held in terms of positions occupiable by singular terms. But it is not a position of this sort which is occupied by the variable 'p' in (1). Expressions capable of standing in the position marked by 'p' are not 'referential' expressions at all but sentences (unless, that is, we adopt Frege's bizarre notion of regarding truth-values as objects named by sentences). It is not clear what sense could be attached to the question whether the position marked here by 'p' was or was not 'purely referential', and it may accordingly be doubted whether the views of these theorists on quantification and opacity have any relevance to quantification of propositional variables of the sort exemplified by (1).

The objection may be pressed by urging that the rationale of the notion of *purely referential position* provides an analogue which does have application to positions marked by propositional variables. The positions from which variables bound by outside quantifiers are excluded are those which give rise to failure of substitutivity. The wrongness of prefixing a quantifier to 'Percy says that x is a fast driver' is dependent on the alleged fact that one cannot substitute identicals for identicals in the position occupied by 'x' without risking a change of truth-value. Can identicals be substituted *salva veritate* for identicals in the position occupied by 'p' in 'Percy says that *p*'? It is not entirely clear what are to count as identicals in this case – the absence of a clear criterion of identity for propositions is frequently lamented.[1] But whoever claims that there is failure of substitutivity in the position occupied by '*p*' will have to bear the onus of providing us with the relevant criterion of identity. Whatever it is, it will not, I think, serve to substantiate his claim about failure of substitutivity. Let us suppose that changing 'Percy says that Mary is Paul's half-sister' to 'Percy says that Mary and Paul have just one parent in common' changes its truth-value. In that case, what Percy is said to say in the two cases cannot be regarded as identical, and we do not have failure of substitutivity because identicals have not been substituted for identicals. The fact is that a necessary condition for regarding 'Mary is Paul's half-sister' as the same proposition as 'Mary and Paul have just one parent in common' is that we can substitute one for the other *salva veritate* in such a context. No analogue for the contrast between purely referential position and its opposite can be found for the position occupied by '*p*' in 'Percy says that *p*', because here failure of substitutivity is the very criterion of non-identity. Referential opacity is intelligible only if a wedge can be driven between substitutivity and identity, that is to say, if we can attach at least *prima facie* sense to the notion of identity without substitutivity. Here there is not even the appearance of a gap into which such a wedge could be driven.

Nothing that the Opacity Theorists may say, therefore, should frighten us out of our conviction that we understand what is meant by sentences like (1).

4

The next difficulty that has been raised takes us closer to the heart of the quantification involved in (1). Dr O. R. Jones[2] objected of a formula relevantly similar to (1) that in order to make sense of it one must regard it as elliptical for

(2)   For some *p*, both Percy says that *p* and it is true that *p*.

He feels that (1) is trying to say that there is some proposition, *p*, of which two things may be said, just as in

---

[1] Without, I believe, justification. *Vide infra*, p. 39.
[2] Jones (2), pp. 27 seq.

(3)   For some *x*, both *x* is old and *x* is tired

it is said that there is some person, *x*, of whom two things may be said, namely that he is old and that he is tired. But (1), it is alleged, does not make clear what the two things are which may be said of some proposition, *p*. To make this clear we have to look at the fuller expression, (2). Here we see that the two things that may be said of some proposition, *p*, are (*a*) that Percy said it and (*b*) that it is true. If, however, (1) is only an elliptical version of (2) it cannot claim to provide an analysis of 'What Percy said is true'. The term we wish to analyse would in this case appear in the full version of the sentence which was supposed to provide its analysis: *circulus in definiendo*.

Logicians think of sentences like (3) as being divided into two parts. The part before the comma in (3) would be called the quantifier (although, as we shall see (*vide infra*, pp. 48 seqq.) it would be more appropriate to call it a quantifier *plus* a variable), the part after the comma the matrix. A matrix – the Latin word for 'womb' – is a container, something with a gap in it, something into which something can be put. The metaphor implicit in the use of the word 'matrix' is thus similar to the explicit metaphor used by Frege when he call predicates 'unsaturated'. This metaphor can be misleading. A container, something with a gap in it, can be contrasted with the thing contained, the thing which fills the gap. Thus the bound variables in (3), the *x*'s which give cross-reference to the '*x*' in 'For some *x*,', are contained by, fill gaps in, two bits of the sentence distinct from themselves, '— is old' and '— is tired'. But of the bound variables in (1), the *p*s which give cross-reference to the '*p*' in 'For some *p*,', only one is contained by, fills a gap in, a bit of the sentence distinct from itself, namely 'Percy says that —'. The second *p* is not contained, fills no gap in any conjunct of the matrix — unless we take it as implicitly framed by what is only written out explictly in (2), namely 'It is true that —'.

Why should we not say that the whole matrix of (1) with the omission of the second *p* itself, namely 'Percy says that *p* and —', is the container for the second *p*, the gap it has to fill? But this would only be putting off the evil hour. For if (1) is, as it stands, a legitimate example of a quantified formula, dropping one conjunct of the conjunctive matrix can hardly make it illegitimate: if (3) were a legitimate formula surely 'For some x, x is tired' would have to be a legitimate formula too? So there can be nothing to prevent our inferring from the legitimacy of (1) the legitimacy of

(4)   For some p, p;

and if (4) is illegitimate so is (1). But the matrix of (4) is all gap, there is no container, nothing to be saturated. The matrix of (4) is as it were nothing but an emptiness to be filled, a capacity to be saturated, a subsistent gap. A feeling of dizziness threatens, as when one tries to make sense of Aristotle's notion of prime matter, pure potentiality, that which is in itself nothing actually but everything potentially, *nec quid, nec quale, nec quantum . . .* etc.

This is where the metaphors of containment and saturation have let us down. It would have been better to forgo metaphor; although if we eschew 'matrix' the only alternative in common use is 'open sentence', which is not much better. Let us start anew, however, with 'open sentence' and define it in such a way as to make clear the difference between it and 'predicate'. A predicate is a fragment of a sentence such that the attachment to it of a name will yield a complete proposition. An open sentence is an expression, part of which is a variable or variables, such that if the variable or variables are replaced by the appropriate constants what is obtained is a complete proposition. In this definition 'part' does not mean 'proper part'. Provided the substitution of constant for variable will produce a complete proposition, it does not signify whether or not the variable or variables constitute the whole of the open sentence.

The possibility that the whole open sentence is composed of variables arises only when we take account of the possibility of employing variables corresponding to syntactical categories of expression other than individual expressions. Substituting individual constants for a string of individual variables, 'xyz', would produce nothing but a list of names, 'Peter James John'. But once variables corresponding to predicative expressions are admitted, open sentences composed entirely of variables become possible. Replace 'F' in 'Fx' by 'is old' and 'x' by 'Joseph', and you obtain the complete proposition 'Joseph is old'. Replace 'R' in 'aRb' by 'is married to', 'a' by 'Charles' and 'b' by 'Henrietta', and you obtain the complete proposition 'Charles is married to Henrietta'.

F. P. Ramsey[1] saw the possibility of this and made use of it to provide an analysis of a proposition which, although it does not contain the word 'true', is equivalent to one which is. Ramsey's proposition is 'He is always right', and this is roughly the same as 'Everything he says is true'. Ramsey's analysis of it is 'For all a,R,b, if he asserts aRb, then aRb'. Again we may argue that if Ramsey's formula is legitimate, the formula obtained by dropping the antecedent from its matrix must also be legitimate. The formula thus obtained 'For all a,R,b, aRb' ('Everything is related in every way to everything'!) has as its matrix an expression totally composed of variables. Here too there is no constant expression which can contain a gap indicated by the variables, nothing waiting to be saturated. But Ramsey's formula seems perfectly intelligible. So it seems that an open sentence composed wholly of variables is quite legitimate.

The trouble with Ramsey's formula as an analysis of the proposition 'He is always right' is, as Ramsey himself saw, that not all propositions are of the form aRb. To obtain a fully general analysis of 'Everything he says is true' one would need to find a form which every proposition will exemplify. Such a form is obtainable as follows: Any proposition which exemplifies the form aRb also exemplifies the form Fx. The proposition 'Charles is married to Henrietta' not only says of Charles and Henrietta that they are married to each other, but says of Charles that he is married to Henrietta and of Henrietta that Charles is married to her. According to the purpose we have in hand we may regard the proposition as being formed either (i) by attaching the names 'Charles' and 'Henrietta' to the two-place predicate '— is married to . . .', or (ii) by attaching the name 'Charles' to the one-place predicate '— is married to Henrietta', or (iii) by attaching the name 'Henrietta' to the one-place predicate 'Charles is married to —'. If we choose either of the options (ii) and (iii), we shall be regarding the proposition as exemplifying the form 'Fx'. This can be generalized: any proposition which exemplifies the form '$Fx_1,\ldots x_n$' (the form of all n-place predicates) also exemplifies the form '$Fx_1,\ldots x_{n-1}$'

[1] Ramsey, p. 143; also in Pitcher, p. 17.

(the form of all $(n-1)$-place predicates). C. S. Peirce put forward the view that complete sentences are those n-place predicates for which $n = 0$.[1] According to our generalization, then, any proposition which exemplifies the form '$Fx_1, \ldots x_n$' will also exemplify the form 'Fx_0'. But this form is none other than 'p'. So, since no predicate can have a polyadicity less than 0, the limit of the series 'For all a,R,b, if... then aRb', 'For all F,x, if... then Fx', is 'For all p, if...then p'.

If there is nothing wrong with the universally quantified proposition 'For all p, if he asserts that p, p' there can be nothing wrong with the analogous existentially quantified proposition (1). It was the matrix we were worried about, not the quantifier. If (1) is legitimate, so, as we have seen, is (4). The limiting case of an open sentence, where substitution of a constant for a variable yields a complete proposition, is the case where the proposition thus yielded is itself the constant substituted for the variable.

Jones's objection has drawn our attention to a distinctive feature of formulae obtained by binding sentential variables with quantifiers. It allows a complete sentence to be built up with nothing more than a quantifier and the variables it binds. The importance of this for the analysis of propositions containing the word 'true' will be emphasized later in this book (*vide infra*, pp. 52 seqq.). But as a charge of circularity against our view that (1) provides an analysis of propositions like 'What Percy says is true', Jones's objection can be dismissed. There is no need to regard the second open sentence in (1) as elliptical. 'It is true that —' is not required as a container before we can make sense of the bound variable 'p'.

5

The final objection to be considered requires us to look into an area of philosophical debate where the waters have been muddied by recent controversy. Proposition (1) involves quantification – hence all our difficulties – and it has become fashionable[2] to distinguish two varieties of quantification: 'objectual' and 'substitu-

[1] See Prior (5), p. 33.
[2] The fashion is due, once again, to Quine. See particularly Quine (4), pp. 91–113.

tional'. Our use of the expression 'For some x,' as a reading of the Russellian '$(\exists x)$' or the Polish 'Σx' already places us amongst the camp-followers of the 'substitutional' forces. Friends of 'objectual' quantification tend to prefer the reading 'There exists an x such that', and the hold that this interpretation has on the usage of philosophers sufficiently accounts for the description of '$(\exists x)$' or 'Σx' as an *existential* quantifier.

The 'objectual' reading of the quantifier makes a difficulty *in limine* for those who wish to bind sentential variables with quantifiers. What meaning can be given to 'There exists a p such that'? Use of the existential quantifier 'objectually' interpreted is said to give rise to 'ontological commitment'. Indeed, it is held to be the sole way of 'committing' oneself 'ontologically'. To bind a sentential variable with an objectual quantifier would on this view involve admitting Propositions 'into one's ontology'.

Binding *individual* variables with a quantifier is thought by contrast to have no such undesirable ontological consequences. 'Tame tigers exist', which is equivalent to the quantificational 'For some x, x is a tame tiger', commits one only to the animals or other objects whose names can meaningfully be substituted for 'x' in the matrix to produce a complete sentence. 'For some x, x is a tame tiger' will be true if 'Havoc is a tame tiger' or 'Marquess is a tame tiger' or 'Goliath is a tame tiger' is true. No one will mind admitting Havoc or Marquess or Goliath into his ontology.

These views about the difference between quantifying individual and sentential variables come rather oddly from philosophers who have seen in the existential quantifier the route by which to escape from the miseries of having 'exist' as a first-level predicate. Following Frege, such philosophers have recognized that 'exist' in, e.g., 'Tame tigers exist' does not attribute a property to objects, but says of a concept that some objects fall under it. Number statements, e.g. statements which give an answer to the question 'How many tame tigers are there?', similarly do not ascribe properties to objects. 'Tame tigers are numerous' does not attribute a property to tame tigers in the way that 'Tame tigers are big eaters' does. We could not infer from the former that Goliath is numerous as we can infer from the latter that Goliath is a big eater. The answer to 'How many tame tigers are there?' may be 'Six hundred', 'Seven', or more vaguely 'A pretty large number' ('Tame tigers are numerous'). It may also be 'Nought' or 'None'. This last answer still more obviously fails to ascribe a property to tame tigers. But what 'There are no tame tigers' asserts 'Tame tigers exist' denies, and if its contradictory does not ascribe a property 'Tame tigers exist' does not either.

These considerations in favour of the view that existence is not a (first-level) predicate are very familiar. Quine's unhappy slogan 'To be is to be the value of a variable' appeared in an article[1] much of which was devoted to showing how the use of quantifiers could free us from a Meinongian ontology. But in our example Havoc, Marquess and Goliath are values of the variable (the tigers themselves, on Quine's use of 'value', not the tigers' names). Being the value of a variable is something, therefore, that can be ascribed to an individual tiger, Havoc. And if to be *is* to be the value of a variable, *being* too must be ascribable to Havoc. But to adopt this position is, surely, to go back on the original *aperçu* about 'exist' being a second-level predicate. The 'objectual' interpretation of quantification seems to take 'exists' in 'There exists an x such that...' as asserting of the x in question *that it exists*. Existentially quantifying individual variables is understood as admitting the objects which satisfy the open sentences containing those variables 'into one's ontology'. To admit an object into one's ontology is to say something about it, namely that it is real, that it 'exists'.

So to understand the 'exists' in 'There exists an x such that...' is not only incompatible with the denial that 'exists' is a first-order predicate, it is internally incoherent. In interpreting it we had to use the phrase 'asserting of the x in question'. But there is no 'x in question'. No answer is forthcoming to the question 'Of which x is it being asserted that it exists?' The trouble with this misinterpretation of the concept of existence is not so much that it treats the verb in a typical existential proposition as a logical predicate as that it treats the noun as a logical subject. Of course the two mistakes are correlative. But it is intuitively easier to see that in an existential statement, particularly a negative existential statement, there is no

[1] 'On What There Is', in Quine (2), pp. 1–19.

answer to the question 'Of what objects is something here being asserted?' than to see that there is no answer either to the question 'What is here being asserted of some objects?'. This *inconvénient* is particularly striking when the existential quantifier falls within the scope of a universal quantifier. Thus 'For every number, *n*, there exists a number, *m*, such that *m* is the successor of *n*' does not conceivably give rise to the question 'Of which number, *m*, is it here being said that it exists?'.

The reading 'There exists an *x* such that...' is dangerous. There are parallel phrases in which the place of 'exists' is taken by a genuine predicable – an expression, that is, which though not here actually predicated of anything could elsewhere be so predicated.[1] 'There dwells in the land of Judah a widow called Naomi, who...' does not actually predicate 'dwells in the land of Judah' of a widow called Naomi, but a sentence could easily be found which does just that. It should not be supposed that the superficially similar 'There exists a village called Oberammergau, where...' licenses the production of a sentence which predicates 'exists' of a village called Oberammergau. The dissimilarity can be brought out as follows: 'There dwells in the land of Judah a widow called Naomi, who...' entails 'There exists a widow called Naomi, who dwells in the land of Judah and who...'; but 'There exists a village called Oberammergau where...' does not entail 'There exists a village called Oberammergau which exists and where...'

These examples show up a further fault in the reading 'There exists an *x* such that'. The ordinary-language phrases on which this locution trades as an intelligible bit of discourse have, in the place taken by '*x*', common nouns such as 'widow' or 'village'. After all '*x*' here is preceded by the indefinite article. But the occurrences of '*x*' in the matrix which follows use '*x*' as a place holder for a proper name. The position indicated by the first '*x*' in 'There exists an *x* such that *x* is a tame tiger' is a position occupiable only by a general term such as 'animal'. The position indicated by the second '*x*' is a position occupiable only by a singular term such as 'Goliath'.

What these remarks are designed to show is not that no sense can be made of the existential quantifier, nor that the 'objectual' reading

[1] P. T. Geach introduced this terminology in Geach (3), p. 24.

is guilty in a way that the reading favoured by 'substitutionalists' is not. The first 'x' in (3) also marks a position occupiable only by a general term: 'For some animal,' is intelligible, 'For some Goliath,' is not. What is being argued is that the reading preferred by the 'objectualists' does not itself specify a way of understanding quantification. By itself it is nonsense, and it may be suspected of actually misleading the philosophers who favour it into remarks about ontological commitment that require 'exist' to be treated as a first-level predicate.

The 'substitutionalists' on the other hand give us an interpretation of propositions like (3) which requires no special reading of the quantifier. They tell us simply that (3) is true *if* a true sentence can be obtained by omitting 'For some x,' and substituting some proper name for x on each of its remaining occurrences (the same for each occurrence). Note that the italicized word in the last sentence is 'if' not 'iff' (the abbreviation for 'if, and only if'). It is thus a sufficient condition for the truth of an existential proposition that we have available a true proposition corresponding to the matrix of the existentially quantified one with appropriate constants substituted for the variables. Quine took it to be an integral part of the substitutionalist interpretation that this availability is also a necessary condition for the truth of the existential proposition. But he and Prior showed that it could not be a necessary condition, since either as a demonstrable truth of mathematics or as a matter of contingent fact there are true propositions of the form '$\Sigma x F x$' where no name 'a' is available to provide a true proposition of the form 'Fa'.[1] Since all that substitutionalists can provide is a sufficient, not a necessary and sufficient, condition for the truth of an existential proposition, their account falls short of being a definition of existential quantification. Prior, at least, is not abashed by this. He is content to accept quantification as a primitive, undefined concept.[2] That is not to say that the substitutionalist[3] provision of an account

[1] Quine (4), p. 95; Prior (5), p. 36.   [2] Prior (5), p. 35.

[3] It is a matter of controversy whether an account like Prior's is properly called 'substitutionalist' or whether that description is appropriate only for accounts which make the condition necessary as well as sufficient. Quine, who introduced this particular piece of jargon, certainly thought of 'substitutionalists' as purveyors of necessary as well as sufficient conditions. He is followed

in terms of a sufficient condition for the truth of an existentially quantified proposition is of no service. Accounts which fall short of being definitions may very well assist our understanding nevertheless.

To bind a variable with a quantifier is not, therefore, to involve ourselves in anything describable as 'ontological commitment'. Philosophers who use sentences beginning 'For some F,...' or 'For some p,...' are not 'admitting into their ontologies' abstract objects called 'properties' or 'Propositions'. The 'substitutionalist' account of such sentences given, for instance, by Prior is perfectly adequate. Worries about what it would mean to say 'There exists a p such that...' are residual confusions traceable to the irrepressible heresy that regards existence as a predicate.

in this respect in his use of the term 'substitutionalism' by R. D. Gallie (Gallie (1) and (2)). Quine, however, implied that the substitutional interpretation and the objectual interpretation were together exhaustive of possible interpretations of the existential quantifier. Accordingly, since Prior's type of interpretation is plainly not objectual, L. J. Cohen (Cohen (2)) has regarded it as proper to call it substitutional. One may hope that in due course, since of the two interpretations Quine discussed the substitutional one is on Quine's own showing inadequate and the objectual one for the reasons given in these pages incoherent, the false dichotomy between the two may be dropped. And the jargon with it. Meanwhile, it is necessary to use the jargon in order to show the insufficiency of 'objectualist' objections against propositions like (1) and thus allow ourselves to get on with the job.

2

Predicating truth

Existence is not the only notion whose status as a predicate has been questioned. Goodness and truth, classed together traditionally with 'being' as *transcendentalia*, have also had their credentials as predicates examined. G. E. Moore marked the difference between *yellow* and *good* by calling the latter a 'non-natural property' – but still a property. R. M. Hare denied that in calling something good we ascribed a property to it at all. What is achieved when 'good' is, ostensibly, predicated of, say, a penknife is that the penknife is thereby commended. Regarding goodness as a property and – what is perhaps the same thing – 'good' as a predicate is, for Hare, an instance of what Austin called the 'descriptivist' fallacy. Not all indicative sentences are used to describe things, to attribute properties to them. Description, the stating of facts, *constatation*, is only one of the illocutionary acts indicative sentences can be used to perform. Some indicative sentences, or key words in such sentences, are not constatives but performatives. 'Good', the most general adjective of commendation, is one of these.

So, according to the early Strawson,[1] is 'true'. When we call a statement 'true' we do not make a further statement: rather, we endorse, or corroborate, or concede, the first statement. The relation between 'This penknife is good' and 'I commend this penknife' is paralleled by that between 'It is true that snow is white' and 'I confirm that snow is white'. The performative theory of goodness was now balanced by a performative theory of truth.

These 'ascriptivist'[2] theories, at least in the simplistic form in which they were first put on the market, were made untenable

---

[1] Strawson (1).

[2] This word for the theories in question, together with the arguments against them outlined in the following sentences, is due to P. T. Geach; cf. Geach (2).

by the reminder that 'good' and 'true' could occur in complex sentences, within the scope of the operator 'It is not the case that. . .' or in the antecedent of a hypothetical or disjunct of a disjunctive proposition. The man who says 'It is not the case that this penknife is good' and the woman who swears 'If what James says is true, I have never spoken to a man in my life' are not, respectively, commending a penknife or confirming what James has said. The constative–performative contrast is a false contrast when applied to the occurrence of 'good' and 'true' in these contexts. The people who utter these words are neither ascribing goodness or truth to anything nor commending or confirming anything. It seems that we must concede that they are *predicating* goodness and truth of penknives and statements in the course of expressing propositions which they are denying or hypothesizing.

2

So apparently there is no avoiding by this route at least the recognition of 'true' as a predicate. The same conclusion is forced upon us by reflection on another philosophical theory which seemed to provide a reductive analysis of truth. Ramsey, in the famous passage of his paper 'Facts and Propositions'[1] which we have already had occasion to notice, remarked that 'it is evident that "It is true that Caesar was murdered" means no more than that Caesar was murdered, and "It is false that Caesar was murdered" means that Caesar was not murdered'. This has been called 'The Redundancy Theory of Truth' and 'The No-Truth Theory'. If it were possible to eliminate 'true' in this way from all sentences in which it occurs, we should have another reason for denying that truth is a predicate. But Ramsey himself saw that this analysis was possible only where the proposition to which truth is ascribed is 'explicitly given'. Where the proposition is 'described and not given explicitly' he held that 'we get statements from which we cannot in ordinary language eliminate the words "true" and "false".' Ramsey's own way of eliminating them has been described in the last chapter (*vide supra*, pp. 9 seq.). It involves quantifiers and variables. 'He is always right' comes out as 'For all a,R,b, if he

[1] Ramsey, p. 142; also in Pitcher, p. 16.

asserts *aRb*, then *aRb'*. This fits Ramsey's description of cases where 'the proposition is described and not given explicitly' because 'He is always right' can be regarded as saying of all propositions describable as 'asserted by him' that they are true. It remains to be seen whether this way of eliminating 'true' and 'false' leaves us with sentences in which anything at all is predicated of a proposition.

3

Ramsey thought, wrongly it seems, that 'we cannot in ordinary language eliminate the words "true" and "false"' from our discourse. Strawson in a later paper[1] did indeed provide an 'ordinary language' analysis – one which had no recourse to the formal devices of quantifiers and variables – of the proposition 'What A says is true', namely, 'Things are as A says they are'. This can, with more or less infelicity, be adapted to cover all cases where the proposition or propositions said to be true are 'described and not given explicitly'. 'He is always right' comes out as 'Things are always as he says they are'. In this paper Strawson was concerned to agree with Warnock over what he called 'the undisputed thesis'. This is the thesis that someone who says that a certain statement is true thereby makes a statement about a statement. What it says about the statement might be supposed to be *that it is true*. If so, the undisputed thesis is tantamount to the doctrine that Strawson undoubtedly *had* disputed in his earlier papers, namely that in saying of a certain statement that it is true one predicates something of it – i.e. that truth is a predicate.

To suppose this, however, would be premature. Strawson argues, first, that even Ramsey's 'Redundancy Theory' of truth, which might seem to render 'A's statement, that X is eligible, is true' as simply 'X is eligible', is on a more generous reading capable of showing the statement to be a statement about a statement. We may, he says, 'entirely in the spirit of the Ramsey-like method' suggest that the sense of 'A's statement, that X is eligible, is true' is given by 'As A stated, X is eligible'. In this, Strawson holds, something is quite properly said to be stated about A's statement. If the absence

---

[1] Strawson (4).

of the actual words 'A's statement' gives us scruples, we can produce a paraphrase which contains them: 'As A's statement has it, X is eligible'.

Whatever its merits, a paraphrase of this sort is of course forthcoming only where the original sentence containing the predicate 'is true' contains also a sentence which actually expresses the statement of which truth is predicated. Only because 'A's statement, that X is eligible, is true' contains the words 'X is eligible' can it even appear to be paraphrased by 'As A's statement has it, X is eligible'. It is when he turns from predications of 'is true' which contain explicit expressions of the statement said to be true to predications where the statement said to be true is not so expressed but merely designated, described or 'referred to' that Strawson has recourse to the formula we discussed earlier 'Things are as A says they are'. He does not notice any *further* difference between the two formulations 'As A's statement has it, X is eligible' and 'Things are as A says they are' over and above this obvious one, namely, that the first contains an explicit expression of the proposition said to be true whereas the second merely 'refers to' it.

The really important difference between these two formulations emerges from an examination of the word 'as'. 'As' in this context at least is a conjunction, but from the point of view of logic it might better be described as a relative adverb (or pro-adverb). This brings out its similarity with words like 'who' or 'which' – words traditionally described as relative pronouns. Sentences containing 'who' and 'which', however, are equivalent to sentences in which the work of these relative pronouns is done by truth-functional connectives 'if' and 'and', and pronouns like 'he', 'her' and 'it', which mediaeval logicians, but not traditional grammarians, also called relative pronouns.[1] For instance,

    (5)   Edith married a man *whom* Alice married

is replaceable by

    (6)   Edith married some man *and* Alice married *him*.

Similarly

---

[1] For the doctrine expounded here, cf. Geach (3), §§ 69 seqq. The linguistic phenomenon of anaphora, which is exhibited by our use of words like 'who' and 'as', is discussed in a relevant way by Grover *et al.*, pp. 83 seqq.

(7)   Edith married Harry, *who* was a butcher
is replaceable by
(8)   Edith married Harry, *and he* was a butcher.
However, the rôle of 'him' in (6) is different from that of 'he' in (8). The force of 'Edith married Harry, and he was a butcher' is no different from that of 'Edith married Harry, and Harry was a butcher'. That is to say, the 'he' in (8) can be replaced, without change of truth-value or sense, by the name it goes proxy for, 'Harry'. The use of 'he' rather than 'Harry' in this sentence is dictated by stylistic considerations only. It is in no way required by the logic of the proposition. Geach calls pronouns of this sort 'pronouns of laziness'.

Quite different is the rôle of 'him' in (6).[1] Replacing 'him' in the second conjunct by its antecedent from the first conjunct, 'some man', would altogether change the force of the proposition. It would very likely change its truth-value. 'Edith married some man and Alice married some man' will be true provided both Edith and Alice are married women, or at least widows. But for (6) to be true the more stringent truth-condition that Edith and Alice married the *same* man has to be fulfilled. This requirement can be maintained by substituting 'the same man' or 'that man' for 'him', but only because 'the same' and 'that' themselves have the rôle of relative pronouns whose antecedent is the quantificational expression 'some man'. 'Him' or 'the same' or 'that' in this context has the same function as a variable bound by a quantifier, a function of cross-reference rather than reference. This point has frequently been made by Quine as well as by Geach.[2]

Just as (7) can be paraphrased by (8), so 'X is eligible, as A's statement has it' can be paraphrased by 'X is eligible, and A's statement states that'. The 'that' in this last sentence is similarly a 'pronoun of laziness', although what it goes proxy for is not a proper name like 'Harry' (which 'he' went proxy for) but a com-

---

[1] There are, of course, connections between these uses of 'him'. A 'verifier' of (6) would be 'Edith married Harry and Alice married him', where 'him' is a pronoun of laziness. Contrariwise an existential generalization of a proposition containing a pronoun of laziness can always be found which contains the same pronoun in its other rôle.

[2] Quine (1), §12; Quine (3), pp. 35 seqq.; Geach (3), §68.

plete sentence. Instead of 'X is eligible, and A's statement states that' we could have written 'X is eligible, and A's statement states that X is eligible'. Here 'that' has been replaced by 'that X is eligible', but the 'that' in the replacement has an entirely different rôle from the 'that' which is replaced. It is a conjunction not a pronoun. For logical purposes it is negligible. In effect the first 'that' has simply been replaced by the sentence 'X is eligible'.

Those who are persuaded by what has just been said will concede that

(9)   A's statement states that X is eligible and X is eligible

– the sentence is a simple conjunctive one so the order of the conjuncts does not matter – has the same force as 'As A's statement has it, X is eligible'. Strawson maintained that this proposition could properly be described as one in which something was said about A's statement. This was his reason for holding that even Ramsey's analysis would allow one to hold 'the undisputed thesis'. The undisputed thesis has, however, been disputed,[1] and one ground for disputing it has been that a conjunctive proposition cannot always be regarded as saying something about an item simply because a word or phrase referring to that item occurs as a subject-expression in one of its conjuncts. Thus despite the fact that 'A's statement states that X is eligible and X is eligible' contains the subject expression 'A's statement' it may turn out that we are not entitled to say that something is thereby predicated of A's statement, other than that it states that X is eligible. And if we are not entitled to say this of 'A's statement states that X is eligible and X is eligible' we shall not be entitled, *pace* Strawson, to say it of 'As A's statement has it, X is eligible'.

4

Consider the proposition 'John is tall and Mary is married'. Are we to say that this proposition predicates something of Mary, namely that John is tall and she is married? Now, if John is short, what the proposition says as a whole is false; so, if the proposition as a whole says something of Mary, it must be regarded as saying something false of Mary. But suppose Mary *is* married. Would

[1] Cf. Jones (1) and (3).

it not then be intolerably strained, despite the fact that John is short, to say of the proposition 'John is tall and Mary is married' that it says something false about Mary? What could it be thought to be saying, true or false, about Mary, except that she is married? But *ex hypothesi* this is true.

These considerations, as far as they go, are persuasive. They seem to force us to deny that every expression formed by removing a proper name from a proposition can, without straining the ordinary sense of words, be said to yield a predicate. 'John is tall and — is married' cannot easily be regarded as producing a *false predication about Mary* when, though John is short, Mary *is* married and the blank in the expression is filled with Mary's name.

I say, hesitantly, that these considerations are persuasive 'as far as they go'. Logicians may feel that they do not go very far. There is something strained, no doubt, in ordinary conversation in saying that someone who in the circumstances envisaged says that John is tall and Mary is married has said something false about Mary. But this need not deter logicians from regarding 'John is tall and — is married' as a genuine predicate. What the logician regards as a genuine predicate is to some extent a technical matter and need not correspond exactly to what ordinary usage regards as felicitous.

There is no need, however, to side-step the objection in this way. One can allow that the conjunctive proposition 'John is tall and Mary is married' says nothing about Mary other than that she is married, without having to admit that the conjunctive proposition 'A's statement states that X is eligible and X is eligible' says nothing about A's statement other than that it states that X is eligible.

Consider the following propositions:

(10)   John married Susan and Susan is Mary's daughter

(11)   Susan's hat is shocking pink and Mary's hat is shocking pink

(12)   Lord Justice Halsbury holds there was negligence and Lord Justice Salisbury holds there was negligence.

Each is a conjunctive proposition, but in each case it would, I think, be perfectly natural to say that something was said by the proposition as a whole of the person or thing referred to by the subject-expression of either one of the conjuncts. Thus part of what (10) says of John is that Mary is his mother-in-law. Part of what (11) says of Susan's hat is that it is the same colour as Mary's hat. And what (12) says of Lord Justice Halsbury is that he concurs with Lord Justice Salisbury in the judgement that there was negligence.

In this last case we have in ordinary English a sentence which is not explicitly conjunctive and which is not only entailed by but entails (12). 'Lord Justice Halsbury concurs with Lord Justice Salisbury in the judgement that there was negligence' is equivalent to (12). 'Susan's hat is the same colour as Mary's hat', on the other hand, is entailed by but does not entail (11). Similarly 'Mary is John's mother-in-law' is entailed by but does not entail (10). In each case there are other possibilities: Susan and Mary might have had hats of the same colour, but aquamarine ones, not shocking pink ones; and John might have become Mary's son-in-law by marrying, not Susan, but her other daughter Edna. But this difference does not seem to matter. What we can say in each of the cases (10)–(12) is this: the conjunctive proposition in question either is equivalent to or entails a proposition which is not (explicitly, at least) conjunctive, and which is obviously describable as saying something of the thing or person referred to by the subject-expression of one of the conjuncts other than what is said of it by that conjunct. If 'Mary is John's mother-in-law', which clearly says something of John, is entailed by (10) as a whole, though not by 'John married Susan', one of the conjuncts of (10), it seems fair to conclude that (10) as a whole itself says something of John. How else could it entail a proposition which says something of John? It is only in virtue of the fact that (10) as a whole says something of John that we are entitled to say something else of him, namely, that Mary is his mother-in-law.

How is it, then, that (10)–(12), though simple conjunctive propositions, manage to say something of persons or things referred to in one of their conjuncts in a way in which 'John is tall and Mary is married', which is also a simple conjunctive proposition, fails to say something of Mary? The answer lies in the fact that more can be said of (10)–(12) than that they are simple conjunctive propositions. (Perhaps their simplicity is thus called in doubt.) In each of (10)–(12)

some element of the first conjunct is repeated in the second. The syntactical category of the repeated element is irrelevant here: in (10) it is a proper name, in (11) a predicative expression and in (12) a subordinate sentence.

Nor is it important for the sentence, if this is the syntactical category of the element repeated, to occur as subordinate in each conjunct. In one of its occurrences, of course, it must occur as subordinate within the conjunct: otherwise we should have a conjunctive sentence like 'Louis is wise and Louis is wise' which as a whole certainly does not say something of the person referred to by the subject-expression of one of its conjuncts other than what has already been said by that conjunct: 'Louis is wise and Louis is wise' says no more of Louis than 'Louis is wise' does. But 'A's statement states that X is eligible and X is eligible' does say something of A's statement other than that it states that X is eligible. And yet 'X is eligible', the repeated element, although a subordinate sentence in the first conjunct, is by itself the whole of the second conjunct.

Like (10) and (11), but unlike (12), the whole of what (9), 'A's statement states that X is eligible and X is eligible', says does not have a special verb like 'concur' for its expression. But the part of what it says over and above its saying that A's statement states that X is eligible is easily expressed. Just as (10), over and above saying of him that he married Susan, says of John that Mary is his mother-in-law, so (9) says something of A's statement which, though entailed by (9), does not entail (9). This can be variously expressed. We may say that (9) says of A's statement that it states something which is the case, that things are as it states they are, or simply that it is true.

In all these cases, (9)–(12), what the propositions as a whole imply about the subject of one of the conjuncts can be given formal expression by replacing the repeated element on each of its occurrences by an appropriate variable and binding the variables by the existential quantifier. Thus

(13) For some x, both — married x and x is Mary's daughter

(14) For some F, both — is F and Mary's hat is F

(15)   For some *p*, both — holds that *p* and Lord Justice Salisbury holds that *p*

express what is implied in this way by (10), (11) and (12) of John, Susan's hat and Lord Justice Halsbury, respectively. And the proposition implied in this way about A's statement by (9) is

(16)   For some *p*, both A's statement states that *p* and *p*.

It is only because an element is repeated in each of (9)–(12) that an existential generalization is possible where the quantifier stands necessarily outside the conjunctive expression. It would be possible also to substitute a variable for one of the expressions in 'John is tall and Mary is married' and bind this variable with an existential quantifier. Thus 'For some *x*, both John is tall and *x* is married' can be regarded as an existential generalization of 'John is tall and Mary is married'. But this is logically equivalent to 'John is tall and, for some *x*, *x* is married'. When we replace 'Mary' by '*x*' to obtain 'John is tall and *x* is married' we are at liberty to place the quantifier either before the whole conjunctive open sentence or before its second conjunct. Which we choose will make no difference to the truth value of the proposition thus obtained. But where there is a repeated element, and the open sentence obtained by substituting a variable for it contains a repeated occurrence of this variable, there is no such liberty. The quantifier must be placed outside the conjunctive open sentence as a whole: placing a quantifier outside just one conjunct will produce, not a proposition, but another open sentence – an ill-formed one at that, because rules for the use of variables would dictate that an open sentence which contained one bound and one unbound variable should have different variables chosen for the purpose. We ought not to write '— married *x* and, for some *x*, *x* is Mary's daughter' but rather '— married *x* and, for some *y*, *y* is Mary's daughter'.

This existential generalization of 'John is tall and Mary is married' is itself a conjunctive proposition, it is one which can be expressed by 'John is tall and, for some *x*, *x* is married'. The existential generalizations we have given of (9)–(12) cannot be conjunctive propositions: the operator having widest scope in (13)–(16) is necessarily the quantifier, not conjunction. If we fill the blanks in (13)–(15) by subject-expressions the propositions thus obtained together with (16) are properly described as existentially quantified propositions not as conjunctive propositions. Conjunction certainly occurs in these propositions, but only as an operator governing open sentences whose variables are bound by the quantifier. The propositions themselves are not conjunctive, as is shown by the fact that no complete proposition can be found which can stand as a conjunct of one of these propositions.[1]

We are thus able to state the rationale for the difference between (9)–(12) on the one hand and 'John is tall and Mary is married' on the other. Propositions (9)–(12) entail non-conjunctive affirmative[2] propositions that are not entailed by either of their conjuncts taken alone. This cannot be said of 'John is tall and Mary is married'. The ordinary language understanding of 'what is said about' a person or thing implicitly makes use of this distinction. A complex expression formed by removing a name from a conjunctive proposition would not naturally be regarded as 'saying something about' the thing named, i.e. as a predicate predicable of that thing, unless the conjunctive proposition entailed a non-conjunctive affirmative proposition not derivable from either of the conjuncts taken alone.

5

So (9) can properly be said to say something about A's statement. So too can its equivalent 'As A's statement has it, X is eligible'. But what it says – or the whole of what it says – is not, as Strawson seems to have thought, that A's statement is true. This is said, not by (9), but by its existential generalization (16). The difference between the two is perhaps obscured by the variant of (9) which employs the conjunction 'as'. The deep structure of some propositions containing 'as' is that of a conjunctive proposition, the deep structure of others that of an existentially quantified proposition. The same is true of propositions containing the word 'who' (or 'whom'). Proposition (7) is equivalent to the conjunctive proposition (8), shown to be conjunctive by its equivalence to 'Edith married Harry and Harry was a butcher'. Proposition (5) on the other hand

[1] Cf. Geach (5), especially pp. 201 seq. (pp. 110 seqq. in the reprint).

[2] This restriction is necessary because propositions of the form Kpq entail negative propositions of the form $NANpNq$ etc.

is equivalent to (6), and the 'him' of (6) plays the rôle of a variable bound by the quantificational expression 'some man'. Proposition (6) is the ordinary-language version of 'For some x, x is a man and Edith married x and Alice married x'. Substitution instances of this and of its ordinary-language equivalent, (6), on the other hand, are conjunctive propositions like (8), and thus replaceable by sentences containing 'whom' where 'whom' has the same rôle as 'who' in (7). But they are conjunctive propositions whose second conjunct repeats an element which occurred in the first conjunct. This is what permits the use of 'whom' in their equivalents. And it means that the sentence as a whole can be said to say something about a person named only in one conjunct. Thus 'Edith married Harry, whom Alice married', 'Edith married Arthur, whom Alice married' and 'Edith married Fred, whom Alice married' all say something about Edith; but each as a whole says something different about Edith. Similarly 'As A's statement has it, X is eligible', 'As A's statement has it, grass is green' and 'As A's statement has it, tomorrow is Thursday' all say something about A's statement; but each as a whole says something different about A's statement. Part of what each of them says is that A's statement is true, but each of them says more than this. None of them therefore can be equivalent to 'A's statement is true', which each of them would entail, and which would say the same thing about A's statement whichever of them were true – whether, that is, what A's statement stated was that X is eligible or that grass is green or that tomorrow is Thursday. What is equivalent to 'A's statement is true' is not any proposition beginning 'As A's statement has it, . . .', but the proposition 'Things are as A's statement states that they are', a proposition in which the syntactical role of 'as' is displayed, not by the conjunctive proposition (9) but by the existentially quantified proposition (16). Strawson was right in claiming that, if 'As A's statement has it, X is eligible' is allowable as a version of Ramsey's analysis of 'It is true that X is eligible', it still represents it as saying something about A's statement. He was wrong in suggesting that what it, as opposed to its existential generalization, says as a whole about A's statement is that it is true, although this is part of what it says.

Strawson moved from his original 'ascriptivist' position about truth to the view that in saying that A's statement is true we are saying something about A's statement. In so far as he gave 'Things are as A's statement states that they are' as a paraphrase of 'A's statement is true' we have no reason to quarrel with him. In so far as he assimilated this style of analysis with that, put forward by him as a legitimate extension of Ramsey's view, which attempts to paraphrase 'A's statement, that X is eligible, is true' by 'As A stated, X is eligible', we see a need to distinguish. The latter attempt at paraphrase does indeed produce a statement which says something about A's statement; but what it says about it is not that it is true, although this is part of what it says.

The acceptable Strawsonian paraphrase is, as we have argued, equivalent to (16). This allows us to go further than merely claiming that 'A's statement is true' says something, predicates something, of A's statement. It provides us with a rendering of the predicate '— is true', namely

(17)   For some p, both — states that p and p.

Attaching (17) to 'Percy's statement' provides us with

(18)   For some p, both Percy's statement states that p and p, which can be seen to be equivalent to 'What Percy says is true'. Expression (17) therefore enables us to say what it is that 'x is true' says about x. 'Percy's statement is true' says about Percy's statement that, for some p, it states that p and p.

6

It is important to note that (17) cannot be regarded as providing a *definition* of '— is true'. A definition must give both necessary and sufficient conditions for the applicability of the term to be defined, but (17), while providing a necessary condition for the applicability of '— is true', does not provide a sufficient condition. If '— is true' is applicable to some item, say, what Percy says, (17) must also be applicable to this item. But (17) may be applicable to an item, say, Percy, without '— is true' being applicable to it. Replacing the blank in (17) by 'Percy' will produce good sense, and may on occasion produce a true proposition. Replacing the blank in '— is true' by 'Percy' will not in general produce a meaningful string of words. If it does, if 'Percy is true' is intelligible because understood as elliptical for 'Percy is a true friend' or the like, its truth will not be a sufficient condition for the truth of the sentence obtained by replacing the blank in (17) by 'Percy', namely 'For some p, both Percy states that p and p'.

This difficulty could be overcome by substituting for 'states that' in (17) some other expression which, like 'states that', requires for its completion into a one-place predicate the attachment of a sentence to its latter end, but which needs for the completion of the one-place predicate thus obtained into a proposition the designation, not of a person, but of a proposition. Two such substitutes for '— states that...' were suggested by me elsewhere,[1] namely 'If anyone were to assert — he would thereby be asserting that...' and '— is the same proposition as the proposition that...' It might be held that '— states that...' when it is equivalent to either of these locutions has a partially different sense from that which it bears when its first blank is filled by the name of a person, and it is only in the former sense that it is to be understood in (17). Such manoeuvres are, however, only of limited interest to us at the moment, because our main concern in this chapter is with the question whether '— is true' can properly be regarded as a predicate. Proposition (17) provides support for the view that it can, because (17), whatever its deficiencies as a *definiens* of '— is true', can at least tell us what is predicated of a proposition by attaching '— is true' to a designation of that proposition: it is the same as what is predicated of it by attaching (17) to a designation of it.

Even if 'states that' in (17) were replaced by, or understood in the same sense as, 'is the same proposition as the proposition that' or the like, (17) would still not provide us with an explicit definition of '— is true'. The reasons for this are similar to those set out in the next chapter (*vide infra*, pp. 33–35), to justify Russell's claim that a definite description cannot be explicitly defined but can only be given a definition in use. It is because (17) does not provide a string

---

[1] In a reply (Williams (2), pp. 58 seq.) to criticisms by Professor Charles Sayward (Sayward (1)). The second of these suggested substitutions, which I owed to Professor Kneale, has since been published (Kneale, William, p. 239).

of expressions everywhere substitutable *salva veritate* as a continuous whole for '— is true'. The point is not the superficial one that (17) as it stands is not a continuous string of expressions but two such strings interrupted by a blank. This could easily be remedied by altering (17) so that it reads '— is an x such that, for some p, both x states that p and p'. This alteration would also take care of the objection that inserting 'Every article in the creed' into the space indicated by the blank in '— is true' produces a proposition which millions accept, whilst inserting it into the corresponding place in (17) produces a proposition no one would accept, since there is no one proposition which is stated by every article in the creed. 'Every article in the creed is an x such that, for some p, both x states that p and p', on the other hand, though unbearably clumsy, is clearly equivalent to 'Every article in the creed is true'.[1] The point is, rather, that if we take, not the simple 'What Percy says is true', but the more complex 'Henry thinks that what Percy says is true', this *may* be equivalent to placing 'Henry thinks that' in front of (18), *but it may not*. It may be intended in such a way as to be equivalent to 'For some p, both Percy's statement states that p and Henry thinks that p', and here the interruption of the string of expressions which constitute (17) is unavoidable.

It is worth observing that this difficulty about providing an explicit definition for '— is true' is not paralleled in the similar case of '— is married'.[2] An objection along the lines we have been considering might be made against defining '— is married' as 'For some x, — is married to x'. 'Every councillor is married' cannot be rendered 'For some x, every councillor is married to x'. But it is easy to use the manoeuvre employed above to get over this difficulty as well: '— is a y such that, for some x, y is married to x' will be substitutable *salva veritate* as a continuous whole for '— is married', wherever the latter occurs. The objection which *does* prevent our treating (17) as an explicit definition of '— is true' cannot be paralleled for '— is married'. This is because the *analysans*

[1] An objection similar to this last one was raised by Professor Sayward (Sayward (2), pp. 101 seq.) to an unguarded claim of mine (Williams (1), p. 122) that a variant of (17) provided an *explicit* definition of '— is true'.

[2] For the similarities between being true and being married *vide infra*, pp. 76 seqq.

of 'Percy is married' contains only one position at which the insertion of 'Henry thinks that' is possible, namely, after 'For some x,'. Inserting it here would produce 'For some x, Henry thinks that Percy is married to x', which is clearly *not* what 'Henry thinks that Percy is married' means. Similarly, 'Henry thinks that' may be inserted after 'For some p,' in (18), and this will not give us what 'Henry thinks that what Percy says is true' means; for on no reading of this is it a necessary condition of its truth that Henry have any thoughts about the correct answer to the question 'What does Percy say?' But this is not the only position at which 'Henry thinks that' may be inserted in (18). It may be inserted before the final 'p'. The difference between (18) and 'For some x, Percy is married to x' is that the matrix of (18) contains an element which is itself a possible argument for 'Henry thinks that —', just as (18) itself is. 'Percy is married to x' contains no such element. It is this syntactical difference between the *analysantia* of 'Percy is married' and 'What Percy says is true' which accounts for the possibility of providing an explicit definition of '— is married' but not for '— is true'.

Unlike the result of our first move in analysing 'What Percy says is true', namely (1), (18) contains a subject term which apparently refers to a Proposition. The only subject term in (1) referred to a person, Percy. It is because it contains the subject term, 'Percy's statement', which corresponds to 'What Percy says', that we can obtain by removing this subject term the predicate (17), which corresponds to '— is true'. The possibility of obtaining a predicate equivalent to '— is true' is dependent on our having such a subject term. If a further analysis of 'What Percy says is true' were to eliminate the subject term, the status of truth as a predicate would again be in question.

What substitutions are legitimate for 'x' in 'x is true'? It may turn out that the answer we have given to the question 'What is truth?' requires modification in the light of the answer that has to be given to the question 'What are truths?'. The bearers of truth are as problematic philosophically as truth itself. The whole truth about truth will emerge only when both questions have an answer.

3
Truths

1

Psychological entities such as beliefs or judgements have lost favour in recent years as candidates for the post of truth-bearers. Debate has concentrated on the rival claims of Propositions[1] and sentences. In the case of Propositions at least it is easier to be persuaded that it is indeed Propositions which are properly called 'true' or 'false' than to have a clear idea of what a Proposition is. My own recipe for dealing with this problem is to turn from general or categorial terms such as 'sentence', 'Proposition' and 'fact' to the sort of expression most likely to take the place of 'x' in 'x is true' in everyday discourse outside philosophy.

In such discourse the vast majority of sentences which end with the words 'is true' begin with the word 'What'. 'What Peter writes in his letter is true.' 'What Jane's mother believes about her is quite true.' 'What Richard has just asserted is perfectly true.' 'What it says on page 74 is true.' 'What Gladstone said in 1888 is still true today.' A. R. White has maintained that the word 'say' has special importance here. He identifies 'the use of "true" (or "false" in which what is true (or false) possesses truth (or falsity)' with 'the use of "true" (or "false") to characterize *what is said*'.[2] There is perhaps an idiomatic tendency in English to associate 'say' with 'true': 'What he says in his letter is true' may sound more natural than 'What he writes in his letter is true'. But there is no necessity in this. What people assume, maintain, suppose, etc., can be just as true as what people say. It is the 'What' that counts.

Before attempting to analyse expressions beginning with 'What' which occur in sentences ascribing truth (expressions which might unguardedly be said to refer to mysterious entities called 'Proposi-

[1] *Vide supra*, pp. xii, note.   [2] White, p. 6: my italics.

tions') we may recall a familiar analysis of expressions beginning with 'What' which occur in sentences ascribing, say, position in space (expressions which might unguardedly be said to refer to material objects). Let us take as our example

(19)   What the postman brought is on the mantelpiece.

Russell would have classified 'What the postman brought' as a definite description, and a Russellian analysis of (19) would be given by

(20)   For some x, for every y, both x is the same thing as y if, and only if, the postman brought y and x is on the mantelpiece.

An important part of Russell's purpose in proposing this analysis of propositions like (19) is to disallow the question 'What does a definite description like "What the postman brought" refer to (or denote)?' Notoriously, expressions of this form can occur in meaningful sentences even when there is no object corresponding to the description involved. Proposition (19) would remain significant even though the postman had brought nothing. The contingent fact that the postman has brought something does not alter the linguistic rôle of 'What the postman brought', does not, as Russell's critics have held, determine the expression as one which succeeds in referring where otherwise it would have failed. It is on Russell's view an 'incomplete symbol'.

Russell explains what he means by 'incomplete symbol' by saying 'Such symbols have what may be called a "definition in use"'.[1] That is to say, such symbols can be defined, but they cannot be defined explicitly. They can be defined only by a rule which permits substitution of another sentence, in which the *definiendum* does not occur, for the complete sentence in which it does occur. It is not possible to find a string of words substitutable *salva veritate* as a continuous whole for the symbol in every sentence in which the symbol occurs without disturbing or altering other words in the sentence.

It is worth examining possible objections to the claim that

(21)   What the postman brought

is an incomplete symbol in this sense. What is to stop us regarding

---

[1] Whitehead and Russell, p. 66.

(22) For some x, for every y, both x is the same thing as y
   if, and only if, the postman brought y and

as an explicit definition of (21)? Expression (22), however, is not substitutable for (21) even in (19) – so far from being substitutable *salva veritate* it does not even leave (19) a well-formed formula. Such a substitution yields, not (20), but (20) minus the last 'x'. This would make the second conjunct of the conjunctive matrix a mere predicate, not an open sentence as required.

We must try again. On Russell's view (19) is equivalent in meaning to (20). Expression (21) is obtained by removing from (19) the last four words 'is on the mantelpiece'. Why should we not look to

(23) For some x, for every y, both x is the same thing as y if,
   and only if, the postman brought y and x,

the expression obtained by removing the same four words from the end of (20), to provide us with an explicit definition of (21)?

The procedure here adopted is highly suspect. It rests on an assumption which Geach characterizes thus:

> if two propositions verbally differ precisely in that one contains the expression E_1 and the other the expression E_2, then, if the total force of the two propositions is the same, we may cancel out the identical parts and say that E_1 here means the same as E_2.
>
> (Geach (3) §43.)

Geach christens this 'the cancelling-out fallacy'. He gives a neat example of a disastrous application of this fallacious principle: 'the predicables "— killed Socrates" and "— was killed by Socrates" must mean the same, because "Socrates killed Socrates" means the same as "Socrates was killed by Socrates"' (*ibid.*).

It would be foolish to allow the cancelling-out fallacy to persuade us that (23) can provide an explicit definition of (21); and (23) can in fact be proved to provide no such thing. It is a crucial part of Russell's Theory of Definite Descriptions that it allows him to distinguish between the primary and the secondary occurrence of a definite description. This distinction shows that we cannot explicitly define (21) just as previously we found that we could not explicitly define '— is true' (*vide supra*, pp. 29 seqq.). If a proposition like (19) is embedded in a wider context, e.g. 'Henry thinks that...', the proposition obtained by similarly embedding (20) in the context 'Henry thinks that...' is not the only equivalent which, on Russell's view, can be found for it. If this were the only way of construing it, i.e. if 'Henry thinks that (19)' were always to be understood as equivalent to 'Henry thinks that (20)', there would be no difficulty: substituting (23) for (21) in 'Henry thinks that what the postman brought is on the mantelpiece' would always be permissible. But Russell holds that this proposition can also be understood as equivalent to

(24)   For some x, for every y, both x is the same thing as y if, and only if, the postman brought y and Henry thinks that x is on the mantelpiece.

Whereas the *definiendum* (21) occurs as a continuous string of expressions in 'Henry thinks that what the postman brought is on the mantelpiece', the proposed *definiens* (23) does not so occur in (24). It is essential to this interpretation, in which the definite description is taken as having primary occurrence, that the words 'Henry thinks that' be inserted between the last two expressions of (23). This possibility is what prevents us from regarding (23) as an explicit definition of (21). This is why Russell insists that definite descriptions are incomplete symbols, that is to say, can only have a definition in use.

An incomplete symbol cannot be a name. A name is essentially a simple symbol, not a string of symbols that can be divided up in various ways and fitted into a wider context now as a continuous whole, now as an interrupted sequence. An expression like (21) cannot therefore be regarded as naming, standing for, denoting, something. It can much more properly be compared to a quantificational expression. The word 'something' does not stand for, name or denote anything. It does, however, share with names the property of yielding a complete sentence when added to what Frege called a first-level predicate: 'Joseph' and 'Something' both yield complete sentences when added to the predicate '— is on the roof'. But 'something' has other properties which distinguish it from names. Like first-level predicates it is capable of being negated: 'nothing' is the negation of 'something' just as 'is not on the roof' is the negation of 'is on the roof'. 'Joseph', however, cannot be negated. Again, certain important distinctions can be made clear only by giving alternative analyses of sentences in which 'something' occurs. 'Henry thinks that something is on the roof' may be rendered either as 'Henry thinks that, for some x, x is on the roof' or as 'For some x, Henry thinks that x is on the roof'. We have here a string of expressions 'For some x, x' which can in some contexts be inserted as a continuous whole in the place occupied by 'something' in a sentence and in others have to be split up so that the second 'x' is inserted in a different position from the 'For some x,'. Just so we found that (23) was not in all sentences substitutable as a continuous whole for (21) *salva veritate*.

Frege regarded quantificational expressions like 'Something' as second-level predicates. He would similarly have regarded expressions like (23). Notoriously, however, he regarded definite descriptions like (21), not as predicates of any level, but as proper names. He did not, as Russell did, think that replacing an expression like (21) by one like (23) would, even in favourable contexts like (19), preserve the sense of a sentence. Oddly enough Russell, who did of course hold sentences like (19) and (20) to be equivalent, persisted in regarding expressions like (21) as occupying the argument position in sentences in which they occurred. Using 'Fx' to represent 'The postman brought x' and 'Gx' to represent 'x is on the mantelpiece', Russell would have written (19) thus: $G(\imath x)(Fx)$. When such sentences were embedded in wider contexts he had to use a clumsy, repetitive, scope-indicating device to distinguish primary from secondary occurrence: using 'H' as an abbreviation of 'Henry thinks that' Russell would have used

$$[(\imath x)(Fx)]H\{G(\imath x)(Fx)\}$$

to express the primary occurrence of '$(\imath x)(Fx)$' and

$$H\{[(\imath x)(Fx)]G(\imath x)(Fx)\}$$

to express the secondary occurrence.

Following a suggestion of Prior's[1] it is possible to avoid ambiguity with a much neater notation by treating '$\imath xFx(\quad)x$' as a

[1] Prior (1), p. 198.

second-level predicate. In this way '$\imath x F x G x$' abbreviates (20), '$\imath x F x H G x$' (24) and '$H \imath x F x G x$', the corresponding proposition in which the definite description has secondary occurrence. Prior's notation is not merely neat. It corrects a confusion which is visibly manifest in Russell's notation. Russell begins with a notation which gives '$(\imath x)(F x)$' (interpreted here as 'What the postman brought') a syntactical status equivalent to that of a proper name. He is here, in despite of his own theory, treating definite descriptions in a Fregean manner as a species of proper name. For Russell, '$(\imath x)(F x)$' like an individual constant 'a', can occupy the argument position of a propositional function: '$G(a)$' and '$G(\imath x)(F x)$' are equally well-formed. But, as Aristotle saw with words like 'Everyone' or 'Someone', this excessive willingness to admit expressions to the argument position of propositional functions gives rise to ano-malies. 'George is wise' and 'George is unwise' are contradictories: 'Everyone (Someone) is wise' and 'Every (Someone) is unwise' are not. 'George is unwise' and 'It is not the case that George is wise' are equivalent: 'Everyone (Someone) is unwise' and 'It is not the case that everyone (someone) is wise' are not. In the case of second-level predicates it makes a difference whether we construct a complex first-level predicate (e.g. 'is unwise') by negating a simple one and then make it, the complex first-level predicate, argument to the second-level predicate, or whether we make the simple first-level predicate (e.g. 'is wise') argument to the second-level predi-cate and then negate the whole sentence thus obtained. In the case of proper names there is no corresponding difference. We may construct a complex predicate by negating a simple one and then make the proper name argument to the complex predicate thus obtained; or we may make the proper name argument to the simple predicate and then negate the whole sentence thus obtained: the result is the same either way. An operator like 'Henry thinks that' is analogous in this respect to negation. It doesn't matter whether we think of '$H G a$' as bracketed thus: '$H(G a)$', or thus: '$(H G)a$'. '$H G a$' is unambiguous as it stands. Not so, as Russell saw, '$H G(\imath x)(F x)$'. But Russell's attempt to disambiguate this expres-sion leaves the definite description, idly, in the argument position, as though this way of construing it was unconnected with the ambiguity. It is as though the quantifier were originally treated as argument to the first-level predicate and might conveniently be symbolized thus: '$F(\Sigma x)$', and only later, when ambiguity showed itself in the more complex expression '$NF(\Sigma x)$', was it decided to disambiguate the complex expression by re-introducing 'Σx' as a scope-indicator, so that '$\Sigma x NF(\Sigma x)$' could be distinguished from '$N\Sigma x F(\Sigma x)$'. But here, as familiarity makes obvious to us, the second 'Σ' is redundant. All we need is a bound variable to indicate, as is necessary only when we have multiple quantification, which argument position is subject to which quantifier. Similarly, all that Russell needed in the argument place of '$G(\quad)$' was a variable bound by the prior, scope-indicating occurrence of '$\imath x F x$'. This is precisely what Prior's notation ('$\imath x F x G x$') provides.

$$[(\imath x)(Fx)]HG(\imath x)(Fx)$$

is as absurd a notation as would be '$[\Sigma x]NF(\Sigma x)$'. Russell's use of it indicates that he has not emancipated himself from the tendency to construe 'What the postman brought' as argument to the function '— is on the mantelpiece', as he *had* emancipated himself from the tendency so to construe 'Something' in 'Something is on the mantelpiece'.

3

'Something' in 'Something is on the mantelpiece' does not name, denote or refer to something. Neither, on a true understanding of the Russellian view, does 'What the postman brought'. What postmen typically bring are letters, but that does not make it legitimate to say that 'What the postman brought' refers to a letter. I am going to argue that the question 'What sort of thing is being called true in "What Percy says is true"?' is as ill-constructed as, on Russell's view, would be the question 'What sort of thing is being said to be on the mantelpiece in "What the postman brought is on the mantelpiece"?'

This will proceed via an analysis of 'What Percy says is true' which is more elaborate than the version given in Chapter 1, namely

(25)   For some p, for every q, both the proposition that p is the same proposition as the proposition that q if, and only if, Percy says that q and p.

The elaboration by comparison with (1) is due to a need to provide for the uniqueness of what Percy says. Strictly, (1) only says that Percy says something true. He may also be saying a lot that is false. (25) does not leave open the possibility that Percy is saying many different things, nor that he is saying anything false. It thus reflects more accurately what is intended by 'What Percy says is true'.

The uniqueness of what Percy says was also provided for by the formula (18) arrived at at the end of Chapter 2. 'Percy's statement' seems intended to refer to one particular thing that Percy says. But the analysis we have now arrived at, (25), is designed to cope with the problem left untouched in Chapter 2, namely, what sort of thing is it that is called 'true'. It is precisely because trouble has been found in establishing the true nature of statements, Propositions, beliefs, etc., that this further analysis has been necessary.

A problem that may be thought to arise about (25) is how we are to interpret the locution 'the proposition that p is the same proposition as the proposition that q'. This formulation, which is due to Prior, has been defended by him in various places in his writings.[1] It will be assumed here that his defence is successful and the locution he favoured for the expression of propositional identity will be used without scruple.

The first point to be made about (25) is that it is isomorphic with (20). There is this much analogy between 'What Percy says' and 'What the postman brought'. Both, on this view, are incomplete symbols. There is no continuous string of expressions simply substitutable in every true sentence *salva veritate* for 'What Percy says'. Analogously with (22) we may try whether

> (26) For some p, for every q, both the proposition that p is the same proposition as the proposition that q if, and only if, Percy says that q and

will provide us with an explicit definition of 'What Percy says', but again the suggestion fails: substituting (26) for 'What Percy says' in 'What Percy says is true' yields, not (25), but an ill-formed expression ending in the words 'and is true', where nothing can be

---

[1] Prior (5), Chapter 4; Prior (1), pp. 190 seqq.; Prior (4), pp. 97 seq., 100 seq.

supplied from the context to be the grammatical subject of 'is true'. So much for the result of substituting the attempted *definiens* for the *definiendum*. If anything, an odder result is obtained by substituting the *definiendum* for the *definiens* as it occurs in (25). Doing this would produce the unintelligible string of expressions 'What Percy says p'. Clearly (26) is a non-starter as an explicit definition of 'What Percy says'.

The analogy of (23) would produce as an attempted explicit definition of 'What Percy says' nothing less than (25) itself. We should thus have the weird phenomenon of a single string of expressions, (25), which purported to be synonymous both with the complete sentence 'What Percy says is true' and with a frag-ment of that sentence 'What Percy says'. There seems to be no candidate for explicit definition of *this* string of words, 'What Percy says', which is substitutable for it in any, let alone in every, con-text. The analogy with (23) breaks down all too quickly. Expres-sion (23) could after all be substituted for (21) in (19) *salva veritate*: such substitution yielded the Russellian equivalent of (19), namely (20). The attempt to produce an explicit definition of 'What Percy says' along these lines collapses *in limine*.

The failure of this analogy is instructive in more ways than one, and these ways are worth examining. But before we look at differ-ences between 'What the postman brought' and 'What Percy says', we can at least note that both are properly called incomplete symbols. The reasons for calling 'What Percy says' an incomplete symbol, in so far as they differ from those for calling 'What the postman brought' an incomplete symbol, are more rather than less cogent reasons for so calling it. And so all the Russellian reasons for rejecting the question 'What is it that the phrase "What the postman brought" refers to, names or denotes?' are at least as good reasons for rejecting the question 'What is it that the phrase "What Percy says" refers to, names or denotes?' Battles over whether 'What Percy says' refers to a Proposition, a sentence-type, a sen-tence-token or an utterance are thus mere shadow-boxing. We should not be arguing for one answer to the question rather than another: we should recognize the question as inappropriate. Since it is an incomplete symbol, 'What Percy says' is not a name; and so, like 'What the postman brought' and, for that matter, 'Something', it is not the name of something.

4

The differences between 'What the postman brought' and 'What Percy says' are, however, equally important if we are to answer, or cease to ask, the question 'What sort of things do we call true?' Russell invented a notation which allowed an expression like '$(\imath x)(Fx)$' to symbolise 'What the postman brought'. We saw earlier, following Prior, that a more perspicuous notation could be constructed which displayed the character of definite descriptions as what Frege called second-level predicates. Thus instead of '$(\imath x)(Fx)$' which Russell allowed to occupy the argument position in expressions like '$G(\ )$', we should have the expression '$\imath x Fx(\ )x$' which would take predicative expressions like 'G' as its own argument. '$\imath x Fx Gx$' is intended by Prior (*vide supra*, p. 36) as an abbreviation of '$\Sigma x \Pi y KE \imath xy Fy Gx$', which itself is the symbolic shorthand for (20), and '$\imath x Fx(\ )x$' may similarly be regarded as an abbreviation of '$\Sigma x \Pi y KE \imath xy Fy(\ )x$'. If we use '$Jp$' as an abbreviation for 'Percy says that p' we may symbolize (25) as '$\Sigma p \Pi q KE Ipq Jqp$' (allowing '$Ipq$' to do duty for 'The proposition that p is the same proposition as the proposition that q'). This again may be abbreviated in Prior's style as '$\imath p Jpp$'. But whereas we were able to see '$\imath x Fx Gx$' as the result of supplying 'G' as argument to the second-level function '$\imath x Fx(\ )x$' there is no analogous way of dividing '$\imath p Jpp$' into function and argument. '$\imath p Jpp$' is obtained, not so much by filling up the place indicated by the empty parenthesis in '$\imath p Jp(\ )p$', as by removing the parenthesis and closing up the space. It would of course be possible to obtain a complete sentence by supplying an argument for the function '$\imath p Jp(\ )p$'. Let 'Dp' abbreviate 'Pauline believes that p'. '$\imath p Jp Dp$' can then be taken as the symbolic equivalent of 'What Percy says is believed by Pauline'. This, after all, is analysable on the lines we are adopting as 'For some p, for every q, both the proposition that p is the same proposition as the proposition that q if, and only if, Percy says that q and Pauline believes that p', i.e. '$\Sigma p \Pi q KE Ipq Jq Dp$'. It is important here to refrain from calling

'$\imath pJp(\quad)p$' a second-level *predicate*, because there are good reasons, which we shall be going into later, for denying that '$D(\quad)$', i.e. 'Pauline believes that — ' is a predicate. But it is legitimate, in a loose but well-established sense of 'function', to call '$\imath pJp(\quad)p$' a second-level function. It can take as argument an expression like '$D(\quad)$' which itself expresses a function.

'What Percy says is believed by Pauline' is the result of supplying 'D' as argument to the function '$\imath pJp(\quad)p$'. 'What the postman brought is on the mantelpiece' is the result of supplying 'G' as argument to the function '$\imath xFx(\quad)x$'. Despite the syntactical differences between these two constructions they are clearly isomorphic. In each case we have in the symbolic *analysans* something which corresponds to the grammatical subject-expression (introduced by 'What...') and something else which corresponds to the grammatical predicate ('— is on the mantelpiece', '— is believed by Pauline'). Untutored parsing may mistakenly treat 'What the postman brought' and 'What Percy says' as arguments to the functions 'is on the mantelpiece' and 'is believed by Pauline', respectively, rather than *vice versa*; but that there is a distinction between function and argument is clear in both cases, even to the untutored, and is reflected in the symbolism. We have the elements '$\imath xFx(\quad)x$' and '$\imath pJp(\quad)p$', on the one hand, and 'G' and 'D', on the other.

5

The symbolic representation of 'What Percy says is true', however, does not allow us in this way to separate function from argument. The same string of symbols '$\imath pJp...p$' which corresponded to 'What Percy says' in 'What Percy says is believed by Pauline' suffice by themselves (with the gap closed up) to do the work of the entire sentence 'What Percy says is true'. To put the same point another way, to change '$\imath pJpp$' ('What Percy says is true') into '$\imath pJpDp$' ('What Percy says is believed by Pauline') all we have to do is insert 'D' between the last two variables: we do not have to remove anything. There is a clear sense in which 'D' represents the quasi-predicate 'is believed by Pauline': there seems to be nothing at all representing the quasi-predicate 'is true'. Truth seems to have evaporated in our analysis.

6

The apparent evaporation of truth is something that has been remarked before this in the history of philosophers' theorizings about truth. According to Ramsey's Redundancy Theory of Truth 'It is true that Caesar was murdered' says no more than 'Caesar was murdered'. But while the complex expression 'It is true that —' can be shown to be redundant in this way, the simpler expression '— is true', as in 'Everything he says is true', has been harder to get rid of. William Kneale gave an elegant explanation of this

> We need the adjective 'true' because we have designations of propositions and require also some way of saying by use of them what could only be said otherwise by means of expressions for the same propositions. If we think of the English word 'that' as a prefix which converts an expression of a proposition into a designation, we may perhaps say that addition of the phrase 'is true' reverses the operation. For when the two occur together they add nothing to what Frege would call the content of the utterance in which they appear, and we are inclined to say that the complex sign 'it is true that' serves only the same rhetorical purpose as the particle 'indeed', i.e. that of indicating a concession or marking the end of a dispute. We must not forget, however, that the word 'true' is often applied to propositions which have not been designated by clauses beginning with 'that' and sometimes could not be so designated by us now. Thus it has been said: 'Whatever a Pope may at any time declare *ex cathedra* concerning faith or morals is true.' Obviously the word 'true' cannot be eliminated from this context by the simple device of formulating expressions for all the papal pronouncements that may ever be made. But it can be eliminated nevertheless by a suitable use of propositional variables, as for example in the paraphrase, 'If a Pope speaking of faith or morals *ex cathedra* declares that p, then p'. And when this is done, it becomes clear that here too the role of the word 'true' is to provide a connexion between propositional designations and propositional expressions. For just as the letter 'p' in the apodosis of our new sentence marks a gap which may be filled by a propositional expression,

so the phrase 'that p' in the protasis is a sign which would be converted into a propositional designation by substitution of a propositional expression for the letter 'p'.

(Kneale, William and Martha, pp. 585 seq.)

When Kneale says that the word 'that' converts an expression of a Proposition into a designation and the addition of the phrase 'is true' reverses the operation, so that the complex sign 'it is true that' appears merely rhetorical, i.e. redundant, he has in mind mathematical analogues like 'the square of the square root of' or 'the half of the double of'. Here the functions 'x^2' and '$x/2$' are the converses of the functions '$\sqrt{x}$' and '$2x$', respectively, and the value of the converse of a given function for the value of that function for a given argument is in general the same as the argument itself.

It is not clear that the analogy works perfectly. Whilst it is plausible to hold that 'that' prefixed to a sentence converts the expression of a Proposition into a designation of that Proposition, it does not seem that adding 'is true' to, e.g., 'What Percy says' converts a designation of a Proposition into an expression of that Proposition. Someone who says 'What Percy says is true' does not, and may indeed be taking good care not to, express the Proposition which Percy expressed by his utterance. He does of course, if he actually asserts that what Percy says is true, commit himself to whatever Percy committed himself to by saying what he did say; but an operation which converts a form of words appropriate to designating a Proposition into a form of words appropriate to committing the speaker to whatever is asserted by means of that Proposition is not precisely the *converse* of an operation which converts the expression of a Proposition into a designation of it. And in any case, the notion of a 'designation of a Proposition' is one which it is the whole purpose of this chapter to call in question.

The great importance of Kneale's remarks, however, lies in his deflecting philosophers' attention from sentences like 'It is true that Caesar was murdered' to sentences like 'Whatever the Pope says is true' or 'What Percy says is true'. It is in sentences of this type that the word 'true' is essential and not simply eliminable. Its use in sentences like 'It is true that Caesar was murdered' is by contrast degenerate and superfluous. Although the analogy between 'It is true that' and '$(\sqrt{}\ )^2$' is not exact, it may at least be granted that the enterprise of seeking an understanding of the concept *true* by considering only sentences introduced by 'It is true that' is doomed to failure in the same way as would be an attempt to understand the concept *square* which looked only at phrases introduced by 'The square of the square-root of'.

The key to understanding the use of 'true' in sentences like 'What Percy says is true' is to see such sentences as ordinary-language equivalents of sentences which contain quantifiers binding sentential variables. Kneale shows himself aware of this. But quantifiers binding sentential variables are needed to gain understanding of the structure of any sentence containing expressions like 'What Percy says', expressions which we might unguardedly speak of as 'referring to' Propositions, or as constituting, in Kneale's phrase, 'designations of Propositions'. The formula '$\imath p J p (\quad) p$' gives us what might be called 'the general form' of the class of *all* propositions involving such 'designations of Propositions': the sub-class which also contains 'is true' is taken care of, not by adding something specific to the formula, but, as has been remarked, by subtracting something, if only a gap, from the formula. This is the phenomenon of the evaporation of truth which we were considering before the mention of Kneale.

7

Dr O. R. Jones has made a suggestion[1] which would involve reversing the Kneale order of the logical priority of 'is true' over 'It is true that'. On Jones's principle, in giving the analysis of 'What Percy says is true' we should not move directly to '$\imath p J p p$', but should halt first at '$\imath p J p T p$', where '$T p$' abbreviates 'It is true that p'. (This is an abbreviation of a modified version of (2), modified, in the same way as (25) modifies (1), to take care of the uniqueness of 'What Percy says'). It will then be possible, in accordance with Ramsey's Redundancy Theory, to eliminate 'T' from '$\imath p J p T p$' in exactly the same way as we eliminate 'It is true that' from 'It is true

---

[1] Jones (3), pp. 108–110. Jones's suggestion was prompted in part by his difficulty in understanding the idea of an open sentence composed wholly of variables, *vide supra*, pp. 6 seqq.

that Caesar was murdered'. The radical sense of 'true', on this account, is given by our understanding its use in the grammatically complex, but logically simple, expression 'It is true that' which may be regarded as the identity truth-function. The analysis which involves quantifiers binding sentential variables is important only in so far as it transforms a statement like 'What Percy says is true' into a form which provides an argument for an operator on sentences. 'It is true that what Percy says' is ill-formed: (2) and the more accurate though complicated version abbreviated to '$\eta pJpTp$' are well-formed.

Jones's theory is attractive in so far as it treats what I have called the phenomenon of the evaporation of truth (the lack of anything in '$\eta pJpp$' corresponding to 'is true' as 'D' corresponds to 'is believed by Pauline' in '$\eta pJpDp$') as the same phenomenon as the eliminability of 'It is true that' from 'It is true that Caesar was murdered'. We do not, on this view, need a new theory to explain the evaporation of truth: the old Redundancy Theory provides us with all the explanation we need.

The trouble with Jones's doctrine is that it does not explain why we have a concept expressible by 'It is true that' at all. What need is there for an 'identity truth-function'? Prior once held that the concept of *the present* was the concept of an identity truth-function like the concept of *truth*, indeed that it was *the same* concept.[1] But in his tense-logic he makes no use of a present-tense operator. The tenses of past, future and present are accounted for by 'It has been the case that p', 'It will be the case that p' and simple 'p'. There is no need to bring in 'It is the case that p'. What needs, other than stylistic or rhetorical ones, are served by the identity truth-function, by 'It is true that p'?

8

Kneale's analysis, taking the occurrence of 'true' in sentences like 'What Percy says is true' as primitive, avoids this difficulty. It provides an answer to the question 'Why does our language contain the word "true" at all?' – a question which the Redundancy Theory, so far from answering, makes more pressing. Of course, an adequate symbolic language will not in fact require any symbol to

[1] Cf. Prior (2), section VI, last paragraph.

do the work done by 'true', just as an adequate symbolism for tense-logic has no need of any symbol to do the work done by 'present'. 'True' is eliminated in the paraphrasing of "What Percy says is true' as '$\imath p J p p$' just as much as in the paraphrasing of 'It is true that Caesar was murdered' by 'Caesar was murdered'. The difference is that the former *analysans* enables us to see why the word 'true' occurred in the *analysandum*, whereas the paraphrase of 'It is true that Caesar was murdered' leaves the occurrence of the word 'true' *there* a mystery.

The need for the word 'true' is this: 'What the postman brought', with reservations noted above when we were discussing its status as an incomplete symbol, does in ordinary language the job done in our symbolism by '$\imath x F x(\ )x$'. In 'What Percy says is believed by Pauline' the phrase 'What Percy says' does more or less what is done by '$\imath p J p(\ )p$'. But in 'What Percy says is true' 'What Percy says' cannot do the job which is done by '$\imath p J p p$', for that job is the job of expressing a complete proposition, of saying something true or false; '$\imath p J p p$' is a complete sentence. 'What Percy says' is a noun-phrase. To make a complete sentence of it a verb-phrase has to be added. The verb-phrase ordinary language provides for this purpose is 'is true'. The word 'true' is needed in ordinary language because the ordinary-language equivalents of definite descriptions demand complementation by something which has the form of a first-order predicate. It would be a mistake to say that definite descriptions have this form in ordinary language because they have the form of proper names or because they have the function of referring to objects like letters or pseudo-objects like Propositions. 'What the postman brought' like '$\imath x F x(\ )x$' can quite well be understood as a second-level predicate rather than as a proper name. Second-level predicates as well as proper names require complementation by first-level predicates if they are to form complete sentences. 'What Percy says' in 'What Percy says is believed by Pauline' is complemented by an expression 'is believed by Pauline' which has the appearance of a first-order predicate. In the symbolic paraphrase of this, '$\imath p J p D p$', however, the expression 'D', corresponding to 'is believed by Pauline', is not a first-order predicate. It abbreviates 'Pauline believes that' which, unlike 'is

believed by Pauline', is an expression capable of forming a sentence
out of a sentence. But the isomorphism already noted (*vide supra,*
pp. 39, 42) between '$\imath xFxGx$' and '$\imath pJpDp$' is such that this syntactical difference between 'Pauline believes that' and 'is believed
by Pauline' is easily overlooked. It is not so easy to overlook the
difference between the surface syntax of 'What Percy says is true',
with its distinguishable elements having the appearance respectively
of a second-level and a first-level predicate, and the deep syntax
of the sentence displayed in '$\imath pJpp$' where no such distinction is
available. The expression '$\imath pJpp$' is capable of forming a complete
sentence either by having an expression like 'D' inserted between
its last two variables or by standing on its own. 'What Percy says'
is not so versatile. Its need for complementation is the explanation
of the existence in our language of the word 'true'.

9

The expression '$\imath xFx(\quad)x$' is a second-level predicate. So is
'$\Sigma x(\quad)x$'. It must have been with some such expression as the latter
in mind that Dummett wrote of predicates of second level 'A quantifier is precisely such an expression'.[1] But Dummett himself, in the
same chapter, remarks that Frege 'freely employs higher-level
quantification'. An expression involving higher level quantification
would be '$\Sigma F(\quad)F(\quad)$',[2] and with such expressions, presumably,
in mind Dummett remarks 'These quantifiers are themselves expressions of third level'.[3] So the identification of quantifiers with expressions of any particular syntactical category would seem to be a slip.
Prior seems to have a more accurate description of a quantifier
when he calls it 'a functor which forms a sentence from a variable
and an open or closed sentence or sentences'.[4] A quantifier with its
variable and the variable or variables in the open sentence or sentences bound by the quantifier may together form a second-level
predicate, as does '$\Sigma x(\quad)x$', or a third-level predicate, as does

---

[1] Dummett, p. 39.

[2] The proposition 'There is some property which all mothers possess', or
'There is something which every mother is', might be taken as exemplifying
the form '$\Sigma F\Pi xCGxFx$'. Here '$\Sigma F(\quad)F(\quad)$' is a third-level predicate taking
as its argument the second-level predicate '$\Pi xCGx(\quad)x$'.

[3] Dummett, p. 49.   [4] Prior (1), p. 198.

'*ΣF*( )*F*( )'. The category of the expression thus formed will be determined by the category of the variables it contains. In particular, an expression formed by a quantifier binding a sentential variable will form a complete sentence: '*Σpp*', which could be paraphrased 'Something or other is the case' or 'There is at least one true proposition', or by Prior's charming 'For somewhether, thether',[1] would be an expression of this kind. To allow Prior's definition of a quantifier to cover this use of quantifiers one must include under the heading of 'open sentence' single sentential variables such as '*p*' or '*q*'. We have in fact already provided a rationale of 'open sentence' which permits this (*vide supra* pp. 8 seqq.). We defined 'open sentence' as an expression produced by substituting a variable or variables for part of a closed sentence, not understanding 'part' in this context as equivalent to 'proper part'. That is to say, we can produce an open sentence from the closed sentence 'Peter swore' either by substituting an individual variable for 'Peter' ('*x* swore') or by substituting a predicative variable for 'swore' ('Peter *F*') or by substituting a sentential variable for the whole sentence ('*p*'). The quantifier in '*Σpp*' thus conforms to Prior's description by forming the sentence from the variable '*p*' and the open sentence '*p*'.

The ordinary-language equivalents of '*Σx*( )*x*' and '*Πx*( )*x*', 'Something' and 'Everything', are often spoken of as quantifiers, and their status as second-level predicates is rightly regarded as one of Frege's most important discoveries. It is easy to think that quantifiers as such must be second-level predicates, as Dummett's unguarded remark shows, or at least to think that the function of a quantifier is, with the variables it binds, to form a predicate of higher level. Such predicative expressions are of course in Frege's terminology incomplete expressions. In the wide sense of 'function', they signify functions and cannot yield a complete expression such as a sentence until supplied with an argument: '*Σx*( )*x*' or '*ΣF*( )*F*( )' is an incomplete expression as long as the gap remains unfilled. '*Σpp*', on the other hand is complete as it stands. It is only if we break loose from the habit of regarding such ordinary-language expressions as 'Somebody', 'Something' or

[1] Prior (5), p. 37.

'Somewhere', or their approximate symbolic equivalents '$\Sigma x(\quad)x$' and '$\Sigma F(\quad)F(\quad)$', as themselves constituting quantifiers, that we shall be able to recognize without a feeling of strangeness that an expression made up entirely from a quantifier and its attendant variables, namely 'Σpp', can be a complete expression, a sentence in its own right.

A further disquiet is liable to be felt when it is noticed that the same expression which by itself is complete can have another expression inserted in it and the resultant expression be itself complete. Inserting the negation sign between the two variables of 'Σpp', produces 'ΣpNp', which can be rendered 'Something or other is not the case' or 'There is at least one false proposition'. Similarly 'Pauline believes something' or 'There is something Percy says' can be represented by 'ΣpDp' or 'ΣpJp'. We are familiar in logic with the notion of a complete expression, a sentence, being subordinated as argument to function to an incomplete expression, e.g. a truth-function, to produce a further complete expression, a sentence. What is less familiar is the notion of an incomplete expression such as 'It is not the case that' or 'Pauline believes that' or 'Percy says that' being subordinated as argument to function to a complete expression to produce a further complete expression. It might have been thought that it is of the nature of a function to be signified by an incomplete expression.[1] Truth-functions, modal and tense operators, and predicates of any level are incomplete expressions. Not so 'Σpp'. And yet there seems as good reason to treat '$\Sigma p(\quad)p$' as function and 'J' as argument in 'ΣpJp' as there is to treat '$\Sigma x(\quad)x$' as function and 'F' as argument in 'ΣxFx'. Nor does there seem to be any good reason to treat '$\Sigma p(\quad)p$' as a different expression from 'Σpp'. Perhaps it is misleading to place empty parentheses between the two variables of 'Σpp'. If we wanted to distinguish the two elements of 'Np' we should not feel obliged to write them as '$N(\quad)$' and '$(\quad)p$'. Indeed it is essential to a logic of truth-functions to identify the 'p' that occurs in 'Np' with 'p'

[1] There may be uses of 'function' which make this view of the nature of functions unavoidable. I believe that there are other ways in which 'function' is used which permit complete expressions to signify functions. The word 'function' is perhaps in these contexts more productive of confusion than illumination.

occurring independently. Similarly we can identify the 'Σpp' that occurs in 'ΣpJp' with 'Σpp' occurring independently.

We do not have to admit the legitimacy of quantifying over propositions in order to produce a case of a complete expression's standing to an incomplete expression as function to argument. We may take instead of 'ΣpJp' the proposition

(27) Percy says that grass is red and it is not the case that grass is red.

Here we may distinguish as function and argument 'Percy says that grass is red and ( ) grass is red' and 'it is not the case that', respectively. Taking 'p_1' to abbreviate 'Grass is red' (27) can be rendered in our existing symbolism by 'KJp_1Np_1', where '$KJp_1( )p_1$' is function and 'N' argument. Again there is no reason why we should not identify the expression 'Percy says that grass is red and grass is red' that occurs in (27) with the same expression occurring independently as a complete expression. 'KJp_1p_1', though complete, can also be part of 'KJp_1Np_1'.

We have been concerned in the last few pages to distinguish quantifiers from the second-level predicates like '$\Sigma x( )x$' which they can help to form, to draw attention to the existence of expressions of other categories like '$\Sigma F( )F( )$' and 'Σpp' which quantifiers can also help to form, and to show that when the bound variable is sentential as in 'Σpp' the resulting expression can be complete, a sentence. What is true of the quantifier 'Σ' and the expressions it helps to form is true also of Russell's symbol '$\imath$', as rationalized by Prior. Prior remarks[1] that '$\imath$' is best thought of as quantifier. It is an expression which forms a sentence from a variable and two open sentences. Thus '$\imath$' with 'x', 'Fx' and 'Gx' forms the sentence '$\imath xFxGx$'. '$\imath xFx( )x$', as we have seen (*vide supra*, p. 36) is a second-level predicate. '$\imath FFa( )F( )$', if we ever had occasion to use it, would be a third-level predicate meaning roughly 'The one and only property possessed by a is possessed by ( )'.[2] '$\imath$' with the sentential variable 'p' and the open sentences 'Jp' and

---

[1] Prior (1), p. 198.

[2] This third-level predicate would appear in '$\imath FFa\Pi xCGxFx$' which might be interpreted as 'The one and only property possessed by Queen Victoria is possessed by every mother'.

'*p*' forms the sentence '*ɿpJpp*', i.e. 'What Percy says is true'. But these same ingredients form the expression '*ɿpJp( )p*' which occurs in '*ɿpJpDp*'. '*ɿpJp( )p*' corresponds to 'What Percy says' and '*ɿpJpDp*' to 'What Percy says is believed by Pauline'. There is no reason why we should not identify '*ɿpJpp*' with '*ɿpJp( )p*'. The same expression therefore can symbolize what in ordinary language is represented by 'What Percy says is true' and 'What Percy says'. In ordinary language a different addition has to be made to 'What Percy says' to express the thought that what Percy says is true from that which has to be made to it to express the thought that what Percy says is believed by Pauline. In the symbolic language '*D*' has to be added to '*ɿpJpp*' to express the thought that what Percy says is believed by Pauline, but *nothing* has to be added to it to express the thought that what Percy says is true. 'Is true' seems to have evaporated.

The explanation of this is now apparent. Unlike the definite descriptions of ordinary language, none of which can by themselves constitute a complete sentence, some of the expressions formed by attaching '*ɿ*' to a variable, an open sentence and a variable can by themselves constitute a complete sentence. This can occur if the variables in question are sentential variables. The final variable will in this case by itself constitute an open sentence. As with other quantifiers, the category of expressions formed this way with the help of '*ɿ*' depends, not on the quantifier, but on the category of the variable it binds. '*ɿxFx( )x*' is an incomplete expression: '*ɿpJpp*' is complete. This versatility is nothing to be surprised at. It is a consequence of the obvious fact that variables can be of different categories, including the category of sentence. Definite descriptions of ordinary language are not so versatile. 'What Percy says' cannot constitute a sentence by itself, it has to be supplemented by the invention of the quasi-predicate 'is true'. It is not the evaporation of truth that needs explanation, it is the existence of the quasi-predicate 'is true' in ordinary language. And this is to be explained as a deficiency, as a failure of ordinary language to mirror in its definite descriptions the wide range of categories the corresponding expressions formed by '*ɿ*' can cover.

We turned originally to expressions of the form 'What Percy

says' to see how an examination of their linguistic role could help us to deal with the question 'Of what sort of things do we say that they are true?' We saw that the analogy between '$\imath x Fx(\quad)x$' and '$\imath p Jp(\quad)p$' showed this question to be an improper one. '$\imath p Jp(\quad)p$' no more names, denotes or refers to anything than does '$\imath x Fx(\quad)x$'. But the disanalogy between '$\imath x Fx(\quad)x$' and '$\imath p Jp(\quad)p$' has shown us that it was as mistaken to ask what it was to say of something that it was true as to ask what sort of thing it was of which this could be said. '$\imath x Fx(\quad)x$' needed a first-level predicate to fill its gap in order to produce a complete sentence; '$\imath p Jp(\quad)p$' needs no such filling. It is already a complete sentence as it stands. The gap does not need filling: it can simply be closed up. Thus truth evaporates.

'What Percy says is true' looked like a subject-predicate sentence. It seems that in questioning the status of 'What Percy says' as a logical subject we have been drawn into questioning the status of 'is true' as a logical predicate. Subjects and predicates being correlatives, this might be thought unsurprising. Similar results are obtained by analysis of existential sentences like 'Tame tigers exist', which also have the appearance of subject-predicate sentences. Precisely in so far as we question the status of 'Tame tigers' here as a logical subject we are drawn into questioning the status of 'exist' as a logical predicate. But we would be wrong to infer directly from the failure of 'What Percy says' to be a logical subject that 'is true' cannot be a logical predicate – or, using Geach's terminology,[1] that it cannot be a predicable: no doubt if in 'What Percy says is true' the phrase 'What Percy says' cannot function as a logical subject the phrase 'is true' cannot *in that sentence* function as a predicate, i.e. be predicated there and then of something named in the sentence; but it might, for all we know, be capable in another sentence of being used to predicate something of something named in the sentence. In 'What the postman brought is on the mantelpiece' the phrase 'is on the mantelpiece' is not being predicated of anything named in the sentence: 'What the postman brought' is not a logical subject. But although not a predicate there, 'is on the mantelpiece' is a predicable: in 'Humpty Dumpty is on the mantel-

[1] *Vide supra*, p. 13 note.

piece' being on the mantelpiece is straightforwardly predicated of Humpty Dumpty. We know the explanation of this. Proper names are not the only type of expression which can combine with first-level predicates to form sentences. Second-level predicates can also so combine. If a sentence is broken up into two elements, therefore, we cannot infer that the second element is not a predicable from the mere fact that the first is not a logical subject, i.e. a proper name. The analogy between 'What Percy says' and 'What the postman brought' is enough to show that the hunt for the entity referred to by 'What Percy says' is unwarranted. It is not enough to show that 'is true' is not a predicable, nor to explain its evaporation. To explain this we must look, as indeed we have looked, to the disanalogy between 'What the postman brought' and 'What Percy says', to the difference of category between the expressions '$\imath xFx(\quad)x$' and '$\imath pJp(\quad)p$'.

10

There is a further disanalogy between 'What the postman brought' and 'What Percy says' which should reinforce our unwillingness to press the question 'What sort of entity does "What Percy says" refer to'? Indeed it may be thought to provide a more profound, and therefore more satisfying, solution of the problem of the status of the bearers of truth than our analysis of expressions like 'What Percy says' has so far provided.

The doctrine that 'What the postman brought' in 'What the postman brought is on the mantelpiece' does not name, refer to or denote anything is no doubt true. But a sentence could be found which did involve the naming of something and the saying of that thing that it is on the mantelpiece, a sentence intimately related to the one introduced by 'What . . .' Postmen typically bring letters, but we are not in the habit of giving letters proper names. So let us suppose that what the postman brought was a canary called 'Simon', and let us suppose that it is this fact, together with the fact that Simon is now on the mantelpiece, that entitles us to say that what the postman brought is on the mantelpiece. The truth of

(28)   Simon was brought by the postman, and nothing else
         was brought by the postman, and Simon is on the mantelpiece
is a sufficient, though not a necessary, condition of the truth of (19).

Prior,[1] as we have remarked, called propositions like (28) "verifiers" of propositions like (19). Similarly the truth of

> (29)   Percy says that Mabel has measles, and Percy says nothing else, and Mabel has measles

is a sufficient, though not a necessary, condition of the truth of 'What Percy says is true'. Proposition (29) is a verifier of 'What Percy says is true'. An important difference between 'What Percy says is true' and (19) is therefore this: despite the fact that neither of them itself contains any expression naming, denoting or referring to any object (other than Percy, the postman and the mantelpiece), an expression which does this will be contained in any verifier of (19) but will not be found in any verifier of 'What Percy says is true'.

There is nothing mysterious about this. In analysing (19) we found ourselves using individual variables. In '$\imath x F x G x$' it is an individual variable 'x' which the quantifier '$\imath$' binds. In '$\imath p J p p$' it is a sentential variable 'p' which is thus bound. We might be tempted to express this distinction by saying that in the one case there was quantification over objects and in the other case quantification over Propositions. But this would be misleading. The expression 'quantify over' is tied to the type of quantification where the variables bound by the quantifier are individual variables. What is said to be 'quantified over' is a range of objects more or less restricted. The objects of the range are the objects referred to by the names meaningfully substitutable for the variables bound by the quantifier. Where the variables bound by the quantifier are not individual variables – where, that is to say, the expressions meaningfully substitutable for the variables are not names and do not name, refer to or denote objects – there is of course no range of objects 'over' which quantification could take place. Talk of 'quantification over Propositions' tends to obscure this, and to suggest that there is a range of objects, abstract objects, mysterious objects, called 'Propositions', which are what the expressions meaningfully substitutable for sentential variables name, refer to or denote. The sort of expression meaningfully substitutable for the occurrences of 'p' bound by '$\imath$' in '$\imath p J p p$' is exemplified by 'Mabel has measles'.

[1] Prior (5), p. 160.

Such expressions are sentences, and unless one wants to follow Frege and hold that sentences are the names of peculiar objects such as truth-values, there seems no good reason for holding that sentences name anything at all.

This argument uses as a premiss the doctrine, argued for extensively by Prior, that sentences like the first conjunct of (29) do not state a relation between a person, e.g. Percy, and an object referred to by an expression formed by prefixing 'that' to a sentence, e.g. 'that Mabel has measles'. On Prior's analysis 'Percy says that Mabel has measles' is composed of a name 'Percy', a complete sentence 'Mabel has measles' and an expression of a sort of which Prior has said 'They are as it were predicates at one end and connectives at the other'.[1] Timothy Potts, it seems, coined the word 'relators' for expressions of this sort.[2] I shall not attempt here to rehearse Prior's arguments in defence of this doctrine, but shall merely try to prevent a particular misunderstanding of it.

Prior denies that 'Percy says that Mabel has measles' is composed of a two-place predicate whose subject expressions are the name of a person and an expression designating a Proposition. 'Percy says that Mabel has measles' does not say something *about* the Proposition that Mabel has measles. He is not, however, contrasting statements about *Propositions* with statements about *sentences*. It would, if anything, be even further from the truth to say that 'Percy says that Mabel has measles' is about the *sentence* 'Mabel has measles'. The sentence 'Mabel has measles' enters into the composition of the larger sentence, but as something used, not as something mentioned. The sentence 'Mabel has measles' is no more mentioned here than it is in 'It is not the case that Mabel has measles'. The recognition that the sentence is used here, not by Percy but by the person who says that Percy says this, explains certain features of *oratio obliqua*. The tenses and pronouns of *oratio obliqua*, that is to say, the token-reflexive expressions which occur here, are those appropriate to the person using the sentence, i.e. the person who utters the larger sentence incorporating 'Mabel has measles' or whatever it may be. Thus 'Stephen said that you were ill' reports what Stephen said, perhaps, by use of the words 'Lydia is ill'. I, speaking

[1] Prior (5), p. 19.   [2] Dummett, p. 269.

to Lydia of a time now past, would naturally use the words 'You were ill' to assert what Stephen then asserted by the use of the words 'Lydia is ill'. I am not mentioning the sentence Stephen used, but using, in order to say what Stephen said, the sentence which I would most naturally use to say that same thing.

The difference between 'What Percy said' when it 'refers to' a Proposition and when it 'refers to' a sentence reflects just this difference between use and mention. If I say 'What Percy said was not fit for your ears' the 'verifier' of this may be 'Percy said "They were a lot of bl**d* s*ds"', and such language is not fit for your ears'. If I say 'What Percy said was quite justified' the verifier of *this* may be 'Percy said that they were a lot of bl**d* s*ds, and he was quite justified in saying so'. The sentence mentioned in order to be described as bad language in the first 'verifier' is used in the second. Those who believe that bad language should be neither used nor mentioned will feel inhibited from using either of these verifiers. But the difference between what they intend to 'refer to' by the use of 'What Percy said' in the two sentences cannot be explained by someone who insists on sparing our blushes in this way. The only way to clarify the difference is to produce such verifiers and note that the subordinate sentence is used in one and mentioned in the other. This is the transparent sense behind the opaque talk of 'reference' to such mysterious 'objects' as sentences and Propositions.

In the same place as that in which he introduces the notion of a 'verifier' of a statement involving a definite description Prior suggests a distinction between what a sentence is *directly about* and what a sentence is *indirectly about*.[1] Having said that 'The present king of Sweden is bald' might be *verified* by the circumstance that Gustav VI is bald, he remarks

> We could say if we like that this sentence is *indirectly about* Gustav, but not *directly about* him, it being understood that what a sentence is directly about enters into its very meaning, whereas what it is *indirectly about* does not. Whether a sentence is directly about anything depends on the form of the sentence,

[1] Prior (5), p. 160. The suggestion is made tentatively.

and in particular on whether it does or does not contain a genuine
name, while whether it is indirectly about anything depends not
on its form but on a fact of nature. 'The King of France is bald'
and 'The King of Sweden is bald' are neither of them directly
about anything, because neither of them contains a genuine name
– neither of them is of the right form – but it happens, as a matter
of historical fact, that 'The King of France is bald' isn't indirectly
about anything either, whereas 'The King of Sweden is bald' *is*
indirectly about Gustav VI.

(Prior (5), p. 160.)

The distinction we are concerned with between 'What Percy
says' and 'What the postman brought' can be made using this
distinction of Prior's. Neither expression is *directly about* anything:
that is the Russellian point we began this chapter by making. But
'What the postman brought', like 'The King of France' and 'The
King of Sweden', may or may not be *indirectly about* something.
Whether it is like 'The King of Sweden' and indirectly, though not
directly, about something, or like 'The King of France' and neither
indirectly nor directly about anything, will depend on 'a fact of
nature'. It will depend in fact on how many letters or other objects
the postman brought, if any. If the postman brought more than one,
or none, it will not be about anything, even indirectly. 'What Percy
says' is doomed to be like 'The King of France', neither directly
nor indirectly about anything; but it is doomed to be like this, not
because 'it happens, as a matter of historical fact,' not to be indirectly
about anything, but because of its form. Whether or not there is
a proposition like (28) whose truth makes it a verifier of (19) is
a matter of fact. If (28) does verify (19), (19) will be indirectly about
Simon because (28) is directly about Simon. But the only sort of
verifier 'What Percy says is true' could have would be a proposition
like (29), and it is Prior's contention that propositions like (29)
are not directly (or indirectly) about anything at all except Percy
and Mabel – and Percy and Mabel are not candidates for being what
'What Percy says' is indirectly about.
  This terminology of 'directly about' and 'indirectly about' does
not add anything to our understanding of the difference between

the rôle of 'What the postman brought' and that of 'What Percy says'. It merely expresses, in a convenient form, what was said at greater length in our discussion of the categorial difference between '$\imath x F x(\quad)x$' and '$\imath p J p(\quad)p$'. It does, however, spotlight the connection between Prior's doctrine about the correct analysis of sentences like 'Percy says that Mabel has measles' and our doctrine that there are no entities over which the quantifier in '$\imath p J p p$' can be said to range. A sentence containing a definite description is, according to Prior, *indirectly about x*, if, and only if, some verifier of the sentence is *directly about x*. Prior teaches that no verifier of a sentence of the same form as '$\imath p J p p$' will be directly about anything named by an expression occupying the positions indicated by the variable 'p'. Expressions occupying such positions just are not names. If Prior's doctrine is correct there cannot be anything other than Percy for 'What Percy says is true' to be, even indirectly, about.

A last point to be made about the 'bearers' of truth is that the doctrine here set out undercuts the dispute between those who would make *beliefs* or *judgements* or *assertions* and those who make *Propositions* the 'bearers' of truth. An expression which apparently refers to something of which truth is apparently predicated will be representable in our symbolism by something which has the same form as '$\imath p J p(\quad)p$'. 'J' here is an abbreviation for 'Percy says that'. But it might just as well have abbreviated 'Margaret believes that', 'Paul judges that' or 'Richard asserts that'. Disputes about whether what people believe are Propositions (and thus classifiable as 'true' or 'false'), or whether they are the same as what people judge or assert or say, are entirely empty. These are not descriptions which may or may not describe the same objects. A proposition which begins 'What Richard asserts . . . ' will be true if some proposition beginning 'Richard asserts that p . . .', with a sentence substituted for p, is true; and similarly for 'What Paul judges . . . ' or 'What Margaret believes . . . ' We may even be moved to say that what Margaret believes is a fact on the grounds that Margaret believes that Susan is her mother and it is a fact that Susan is her mother. But it would be silly to argue from this that some beliefs were facts whilst others were merely Propositions. Expressions of the form '$\eta p J p(\quad)p$' are not either directly or indirectly about objects so there is no room for argument over what sort of object any particular expression of this form is about.

Philosophers who have regarded beliefs or assertions or judgements as bearers of truth in preference to Propositions have probably done so because they regarded the former as concrete mental or physical states or events and the latter as abstract objects. But it would in any case be a mistake to interpret 'Margaret's belief' in 'Margaret's belief is true' as referring to a mental state. 'Margaret's belief' here means 'What Margaret believes', not 'Margaret's believing'. What Margaret believes may be the same as what you and I believe (if, for some p, Margaret believes that p and you believe that p and I believe that p), but Margaret's believing it and your believing it and my believing it are quite different from each other. (Margaret's belief and mine, in the latter sense, may be due to childhood indoctrination whereas yours is the result of adult conversion.) But our argument shows that the assignment of the rôle of truth-bearers to mental states was not only mistaken but unnecessary. Abstract objects can be avoided even though Margaret's belief is not her believing but what she believes. Since 'What Margaret believes' is not directly or indirectly about objects, it is not about abstract objects either.

4
Falsehoods

It has been objected against Plato and Descartes that their epistemologies are faulty because they construct theories of knowledge which leave no room for a theory of error. If to know something is to be related in some way to a Form, or to a clear and distinct idea, the only alternative to being so related is not being so related, and that will be ignorance, not error. Conceiving the objects of knowledge as something simple, these philosophers made no allowance for the possibility of someone's mistakenly believing that he knew something. For, as Ryle[1] once pointed out, a simple object (like the number Seven) can never by itself be the object of a mistaken belief.

Theories of Truth ought, by analogy, to beware of leaving no room for a Theory of Falsehood. If something is put forward as an analysis of a statement like 'What Percy says is true', we must ask what analysis on similar lines could be provided for 'What Percy says is false'. It will count against the proposed analysis of truth if the corresponding analysis of falsehood is less than convincing.

Our present position is that (25), of which '$\imath p J p p$' is the symbolic abbreviation, is a satisfactory analysis of 'What Percy says is true'. It would appear to follow that the negation of this, namely '$N\imath p J p p$', must be equally satisfactory as a paraphrase of 'What Percy says is false'. On the other hand, the same considerations which led us to adopt '$\imath p J p p$' as the analysis of 'What Percy says is true' seem to lead to '$\imath p J p N p$' as the analysis of 'What Percy says is false'. After all, 'Percy says that Mabel has measles, and Percy does not say anything else, and it is not the case that Mabel has measles' looks entirely suitable as a 'verifier' of 'What Percy says is false'. But whereas '$\imath p J p p$' and '$N\imath p J p p$' are contradictories, '$\imath p J p p$' and '$\imath p J p N p$' are merely contraries. Can 'What Percy says is true' and

[1] Ryle, p. 137, in the reprint.

'What Percy says is false' be mere contraries, i.e. can they both be false? Must not what Percy says be either true or false?

We have, of course, been here before. These questions are precisely analogous to those Russell asked about the present King of France. Russell's solution would no doubt be to draw a distinction between the primary and the secondary occurrence of 'What Percy says' in 'What Percy says is not true', corresponding to '$\imath p J p N p$' and '$N \imath p J p p$' respectively. 'What Percy says is false' would be equivalent to 'What Percy says is not true' where the definite description is taken as having primary occurrence.

Familiar too is the account which Strawson would give of these sentences. 'What Percy says is true' and 'What Percy says is false' would according to Strawson say something true or false if, and only if, Percy does in fact say just one thing. If Percy says nothing, or says more than one thing, the question of the truth or falsity of 'What Percy says is true' and 'What Percy says is false' does not arise. Less happily, in the light of what has been said in the last chapter, a Strawsonian would talk in this case of the expression 'What Percy says' failing of reference, failing to refer. There are, as we have seen, objections to talking about any definite description's having reference, if by this is meant that a sentence containing it is *directly about* something; and there are additional objections to talking about a definite description like 'What Percy says' having reference, if by this is meant that a sentence containing it is *indirectly about* something. Whatever infelicity, therefore, is committed by someone who says 'What Percy says is true (false)' when the number of things said by Percy is more or less than one, it is a further infelicity to describe the situation as someone's employing a referring expression which fails to refer.

The arguments in support of the Russellian and Strawsonian accounts of sentences containing definite descriptions, and the objections against these accounts, are well enough known. They do not in general require modification to take account of the difference between expressions like 'What the postman brought' and expressions like 'What Percy says'. I shall not go into them here. I shall merely attempt to expound a third account of sentences of this type, an account which seems to me to preserve the merits of both the

Strawsonian and the Russellian analyses, without getting involved in their besetting difficulties.

2

This account of sentences containing definite descriptions is entailed by a theory about a wider class of sentences, a class which includes sentences containing definite descriptions. The more general theory is propounded in Geach's article 'Assertion',[1] but is not there applied to sentences containing definite descriptions. An earlier article by Geach[2] in which he deals explicitly with definite descriptions seems to me to put forward a theory which is generalized by that expounded in 'Assertion'. But Professor Geach does not see the two theories as related in this way, so I must take responsibility myself for so regarding them.

The more general theory applies to sentences like 'Jim is aware of the fact that his wife is unfaithful' or 'Is Jim aware of the fact that his wife is deceiving him?' Someone who utters the first sentence (not as a subordinate sentence, but as a complete speech act) is making in effect two assertions, that Jim is convinced that his wife is unfaithful, and that Jim's wife is unfaithful. Someone who utters the second sentence is not just asking a question, he is also making the assertion that Jim's wife is deceiving him. In the first case we might be tempted to confuse what is happening with the assertion of the conjunctive proposition that both Jim is convinced that his wife is unfaithful and Jim's wife is unfaithful, but the second case, where there is one thing asked and another asserted, ought to preserve us from this confusion. Philosophers have been perplexed how the utterance of a sentence like 'Jim is aware of the fact that his wife is unfaithful' can escape from the Law of the Excluded Middle: for if Jim's wife is not unfaithful neither 'Jim is aware of the fact that his wife is unfaithful' nor 'Jim is not aware of the fact that his wife is unfaithful' is true. But if the utterance of the sentence is the assertion of two propositions, not one, there is no one proposition here asserted which must be true or false: there are four possibilities of truth or falsity, not two.

There is a wide variety of sentences to which this theory applies other than those given so far. Professor Geach attributes to Mr Brian

---

[1] Geach (4).   [2] Geach (1).

Loar an application of the theory to certain sentences containing qualifying relative clauses: if someone asserts 'Smith, who called on the Registrar yesterday, has already resigned his chair' this is tantamount to asserting simultaneously (i) 'Smith called on the Registrar yesterday' and (ii) 'Smith has already resigned his chair'. 'Edith married Harry, who was a butcher' should probably not be analysed, as suggested earlier, as asserting the conjunction of 'Edith married Harry' and 'Harry was a butcher' (*vide supra*, p. 20) but as jointly making these two different assertions. The most familiar example of all is the question 'Have you stopped beating your wife yet?' Use of this sentence involves simultaneously asking you whether you beat your wife and asserting that you used to beat your wife. Any use of the word 'stop' involves an implicit assertion that the person of whom we say that he stops or ask whether he has stopped, or whom we command to stop, is or has been engaged in the activity whose cessation is in question.

The general theory then is that there are sentences whose utterance as a complete speech act constitutes either the assertion of more than one proposition or the assertion of a proposition coupled with some other speech act such as the asking of a question or the issuing of a command. The application of the theory to sentences containing definite descriptions can be made most easily if we look at the version of Russell's Theory of Descriptions in which he analyses a statement like (19) not as an existentially quantified statement like (20) but as a conjunctive statement. On this analysis (19) is equivalent to the conjunction of (i) 'The postman brought at least one object', (ii) 'The postman brought at most one object' and (iii) 'Whatever the postman brought is on the mantelpiece'. The conjunction of these three propositions is easily shown to be equivalent to (20). If, however, the general theory about assertion which we have been expounding has application to sentences containing definite descriptions, Russell is wrong in equating the utterance of (19) to the assertion of a conjunctive proposition of the kind described. Rather, the utterance of (19) as a complete speech act can be regarded as the joint assertion of (iii) and of the conjunction of (i) and (ii). The conjunction of (i) and (ii) is tantamount to 'The postman brought just one object', so we are saying that someone who utters (19) as a complete speech act is making together both the assertion that the postman brought just one object and the assertion that anything the postman brought is on the mantelpiece.

This applies just as well to 'What Percy says is true' as to 'What the postman brought is on the mantelpiece'. Proposition (25), the Russellian analysis of 'What Percy says is true', is equivalent to the conjunction of 'Percy says just one thing' and 'For every p, if Percy says[1] that p, p'. On the view we have been propounding the utterance of 'What Percy says is true' as a complete speech act is tantamount to the joint assertion of 'Percy says just one thing' and 'For every p, if Percy says that p, p'. In our symbolism the two propositions each of which is here being asserted are represented as '$\Sigma p\Pi q EIpqJq$' and '$\Pi r CJrr$'.

The application to 'What Percy says is false' is obvious. Someone who utters 'What Percy says is false' as a complete speech act is making together both the assertion that Percy says just one thing and the assertion that for some p, both Percy says that p and it is not the case that p. This last assertion, representable symbolically as '$\Sigma r KJrNr$', is of course equivalent to the denial of 'For every p, if Percy says that p, p', i.e. to '$N\Pi r CJrr$'.

'What Percy says is true' and 'What Percy says is false' are thus not contradictories. So far the theory agrees with Russell. But the reason why 'What Percy says is false' is not the contradictory of 'What Percy says is true' is not that something else is. According to Russell 'What Percy says is true' is equivalent to a conjunctive proposition. The negation of a conjunctive proposition is equivalent to a disjunctive proposition. If 'What Percy says is true' were equivalent to '$K\Sigma p\Pi q EIpqJq\Pi r CJrr$' its negation would be equivalent to '$AN\Sigma p\Pi q EIpqJqN\Pi r CJrr$'. On the view we are adopting we are not obliged to say that 'Either Percy does not say just one thing or, for some p, both Percy says that p and it is not the case that p' is the contradictory of 'What Percy says is true' – a particular application of a doctrine which was never an easy one to swallow. Rather, we are unable to say that anything is *the* contradictory of 'What

[1] The tense of 'says' here is dangerously ambiguous. It is intended in such a way that a correct paraphrase would be 'is now saying', not 'at any time says'.

Percy says is true'. How could it be, if the utterance of this sentence is the assertion of not one but two propositions? No one proposition could be the contradictory of two propositions that are not equivalent.

We have also avoided having to say that 'Either Percy does not say just one thing or, for every p, if Percy says that p, p' is the contradictory of 'What Percy says is false' – an even more unpalatable consequence of the Russellian analysis.

3

Geach's doctrine as it is expounded in 'Assertion' has nothing to say about any difference between the relations in which the different assertions made by a multiply assertive utterance stand to the utterance itself. In 'Russell's Theory of Descriptions', where he relates Russell's problem about the King of France to the fallacy of 'many questions', he talks about an affirmative answer to one question being presupposed by the act of asking another. He says that three questions are involved in the question 'Have you been happier since your wife died?' (i) 'Have you ever had a wife?' (ii) 'Is she dead?' (iii) 'Have you been happier since then?' The act of asking the second question, according to Geach, presupposes an affirmative answer to the first; if the true answer to the first is negative, the second question *does not arise*. And so with the third question and the second. The third question, of course, *is* the question 'Have you been happier since your wife died?' Similarly there seems to be some relation of presupposition involved in the multiply assertive sentence we have been examining. 'Jim is aware of the fact that his wife is unfaithful' presupposes that Jim's wife is unfaithful. It does not presuppose that Jim is convinced that his wife is unfaithful. To ask whether Jim is aware that his wife is deceiving him is to presuppose that Jim's wife is deceiving him. It does not presuppose that, but asks whether, Jim is convinced that this is so.

So with 'What Percy says is true'. To say this is to assert that Percy says just one thing, but it is to presuppose what is thus asserted with a view to asserting further that, for every p, if Percy says that p, p. There is a difference between the ways in which the two things that are asserted by an utterance of 'What Percy says is true' are related to that utterance.

The same point can be made by considering the rudimentary analysis of 'What Percy says is true' which yields not a conjunctive but an existential proposition, namely (1). This analysis may be compared to the famous definition of truth given by Aristotle in *Metaphysics* 1011^{b}27: 'to say of what is that it is and of what is not that it is not is true'. It does not need a particularly indulgent exegesis to see that what Aristotle intends is to define '*saying* what is true' as 'saying of what is that it is and of what is not that it is not'.[1] Aristotle tends to use the Greek equivalent of 'is' as a dummy verb, very much as we use a predicative variable 'F' or 'G'. In this sense 'saying of what is that it is' is the same as 'saying of what F's that it F's' or as 'saying of what is so-and-so that it is so-and-so'.[2] Now 'Percy says of what F's that it F's' can be represented in modern quantifier notation by 'For some x, for some F, Fx and Percy says that Fx'. (This, incidentally, covers 'Percy says of what is not that it is not'. 'NGx' is just a special case of 'Fx'. If 'G' and 'a' are constants, 'NGa and Percy says that NGa' is a possible 'verifier' of 'For some x, for some F, Fx and Percy says that Fx'.) But more states of affairs may be indicated by 'Percy says what is true' than by 'For some x, for some F, Fx and Percy says that Fx'. Percy may, after all, have said something not of the form 'Fx' but of the form 'xRy'. He may have said something whose expression is not of the subject-predicate form at all. So Aristotle's formula needs generalizing. We have seen how this can be done in the case of Ramsey's

[1] We may thus quickly surmount a difficulty raised by Mr Warnock: 'Aristotle's remark...seems to express the very odd idea that what is (typically, centrally) true is *to say* something' (Warnock, p. 145, note 2).

[2] Christopher Kirwan in his commentary on this passage in the Clarendon Aristotle Series (Kirwan, p. 117) allows that 'is' could mean 'is so-and-so', but opts rather for its meaning 'is the case'. To interpret it in this way in this context, so that 'saying what is true' is defined as 'saying of what is the case that it is the case', comes near to circularity: 'what is the case' is practically synonymous with 'what is true'. Taking it as 'is so-and-so' will restrict Aristotle's description of true statements to those which say of *a* that it F's (when it does), i.e. to subject-predicate statements; but such a restriction is unlikely to have been felt as a restriction by Aristotle, and in any case his remark at 1011^{b}24 asserting one thing of one thing shows that he had subject-predicate statements in mind.

analogous formula (*vide supra*, pp. 9 seq.). The required generalization is 'For some *p*, *p* and Percy says that *p* '.

The difference between this formula and (1) is that in the former the conjunct of the matrix which mentions Percy comes second whereas in the latter it comes first. In these semi-formal expressions this reversal of order is immaterial: conjunction permits commutation. But the sentence 'For some *p*, *p* and Percy says that *p* ' has been advanced as an adaptation of Aristotle's 'saying of what is that it is' and (1) is an attempt at formalizing Strawson's 'Things are as [Percy] says they are'. The difference between these informal versions does seem worth remarking. Aristotle describes what Percy says as saying that *what is so-and-so* is so-and-so; Strawson describes Percy's statement as one of which it can be said that things are *as it says they are*. Aristotle puts into the relative clause (actually he uses a definite description '*to on*') the reference to what is the case, the world; Strawson puts into the relative clause the reference to what is said, to the words. The difference comes out in the quantificational versions only in the order of conjuncts, which in these versions is unimportant. In the informal versions it is important. The opposite of Percy's saying of what is so-and-so that it is so-and-so is Percy's not saying this – which he could do by keeping quiet. The opposite of things' being as Percy says they are is their not being like this. It is the latter, surely, which corresponds to Percy's statement's being false. This gives us a reason, which we could not have if we considered only the quantificational versions, for preferring the Strawsonian to the Aristotelian analysis.

To be sure, (1) does not include 'For some *p*, Percy says that *p* ' as a conjunct. (1) is not a conjunctive, but an existential, proposition – that is to say, the operator having the widest scope in (1) is the existential quantifier, not the conjunctive truth-function. So we cannot deal with 'Things are as Percy says they are' in exactly the same way as we dealt with 'Jim is aware of the fact that his wife is unfaithful' – by drawing a distinction between the assertion of a conjunctive proposition and the use of a single sentence to make two assertions. But (1) entails 'For some *p*, Percy says that *p* ', and in this way resembles the conjunctive proposition 'Jim is convinced that his wife is unfaithful and Jim's wife is unfaithful' which entails each of its conjuncts and, in particular, 'Jim's wife is unfaithful'. Just as it would be odd to say that the falsity of 'Jim's wife is unfaithful' entails the falsity of 'Jim is aware of the fact that his wife is unfaithful', so it would be odd to say that the falsity of 'Percy says something' entails the falsity of 'Things are as Percy says they are'. We have thus a good reason for saying that 'Things are as Percy says they are' presupposes rather than entails that Percy says something, just as we have for saying that 'Jim is aware of the fact that his wife is unfaithful' presupposes rather than entails that Jim's wife is unfaithful.

In Chapter 2 we accepted without question the doctrine, often enunciated by Quine, that relative pronouns are at times the ordinary-language equivalents of quantifiers and their variables. And, since 'as' can be regarded as a 'relative pro-adverb', (1) was taken to be the equivalent of 'Things are *as* Percy says they are'. Frequently, however, the fact indicated by the relative clause is related to the fact indicated by the main clause in a different way from that in which the two conjuncts of the matrix of the quantificational version are related. The latter are reversible without change of sense. The former are significantly ordered. The question whether (1) is true arises even if Percy says nothing: it arises and it is able to be answered negatively. But if Percy says nothing, the question whether things are as Percy says they are does not arise. Nor does the question whether what Percy says is true.

4

'What Percy says is true' does not refer to some mysterious, abstract object called a Proposition named by the phrase 'What Percy says'. But like 'Things are as Percy says they are' it presupposes a fact, the fact that Percy says something. In a sense it asserts this fact, as well as asserting the fact that whatever Percy says is true; only there is a difference between the ways in which the two things that are asserted are related to the assertion that what Percy says is true. What happens when I say 'What Percy says is true' is that I take something for granted, namely that Percy says something, and proceed on this basis to make a challenge, a challenge which would normally be taken up, by someone who rejected my claim, with the words 'What Percy says is false'. Similarly, if I utter (19) I take something for granted, namely that the postman has brought just one object; and if I say 'The successor of 35 is the square of 6' I take for granted that 35 has a successor. Even when I say 'Mabel has measles' I take something for granted, namely that there is a person who fits some identifying description which I might give if asked whom I meant by 'Mabel'.

These considerations echo in some respects points made by Strawson in *Individuals* about what he called 'the introduction of particulars'.[1] If what has been argued above is correct, the fact that the use of an expression presupposes something does not show that expression to be a particular-introducing expression. The use of 'as Percy says they are' in 'Things are as Percy says they are' presupposes that Percy says something, and the use of 'stopped beating your wife' presupposes that you have been beating your wife. Yet neither of these expressions has even the appearance of introducing particulars into discourse. The use of 'the fact that his wife is unfaithful' in 'Jim is aware of the fact that his wife is unfaithful' has indeed the appearance of introducing a particular, but when we consider that the words 'of the fact' can be omitted from this sentence without change of sense we shall be disinclined to call the fact in question anything more than a 'quasi-particular'. Similarly, the possibility of rendering 'What Percy says is true', with its apparent reference to a Proposition, by 'Things are as Percy says they are' will make us as unwelcoming to the idea of a class of particulars called 'Propositions' as we are to that of a class of particulars called 'facts'.

We can recognize, then, that the phenomena of multiple assertion and presupposition are more general than the phenomena involved in the introduction of particulars by definite descriptions or proper names. Nevertheless, reference to particulars is the paradigm case of presupposition, and it is not surprising that natural languages tend to assimilate locutions which involve presupposition to the definite description model: hence the tendency to use the locution 'aware of the fact that' rather than the more simple 'aware that'. Hence too the use of a single type of linguistic structure to cover both cases like

[1] Strawson (3), Chapter 6 ,§§ 2–3.

'What the postman brought' and 'What Percy says'. Here there is a consequent assimilation of other elements in the sentence, so that the operator on sentences 'Pauline believes that' gets transformed into the predicative-style expression 'is believed by Pauline', and a new predicative-style expression 'is true' is invented to indicate, as it were, the closing-up of the gap in '$\imath p J p(\quad)p$'. There are, then, two factors which explain the superficial similarity between expressions like 'What Percy says' and expressions which refer to objects. One is the isomorphism which we have noticed between the *analysantia* of such expressions and the *analysantia* of expressions like 'What the postman brought', between '$\imath x F x(\quad)x$' and '$\imath p J p(\quad)p$'. This makes it natural, though misleading, for expressions like 'What Percy says' to be coupled with expressions which have the style of one-place predicates such as 'is believed by Pauline' or 'is true', just as 'What the postman brought' is coupled with 'is on the mantelpiece'. That this is misleading can be noticed without recourse to the formal apparatus of the quantifier '$\imath$' and the different categories of the variables it binds. It can be brought out by noticing that whereas the 'verifier' of 'What the postman brought is on the mantelpiece', e.g. (28), will contain the expression 'is on the mantelpiece' the 'verifiers' of 'What Percy says is believed by Pauline' and 'What Percy says is true', e.g. 'Percy says that Mabel has measles and Pauline believes that Mabel has measles' and (29), will not contain 'is believed by Pauline' or 'is true'. But misleadingly or not expressions like 'What Percy says' play the same surface syntactical role as expressions like 'What the postman brought', and whatever feeling there is that expressions of the latter sort 'refer to' objects is transferred to expressions of the former sort.

The other factor which makes it natural to regard both these sorts of expression as referring to objects is the presupposition carried by their use. It is also a feature of the use of proper names. As we have seen, I cannot properly use the name 'Mabel' without presupposing some fact which would uniquely identify the woman or girl whom I am calling by this name. Because such presupposition is involved in the use also of definite descriptions, it becomes easy to think of definite descriptions also as referring to, being '*directly about*', objects. Perhaps this is why Frege enlarged the denotation of 'proper name' so that it could be used by him to apply to expressions like 'What the postman brought' as well as to expressions like 'Mabel'. Once definite descriptions which are *'indirectly about'* objects had been taken in this way to be directly about objects, it was not difficult to take expressions like 'What Percy says', which in fact are not even indirectly about objects, to be directly about objects also. The objects they were taken to be directly about were called 'Propositions'.

5

The presupposition borne by sentences like 'What Percy says is true' is real enough, even though the propositional objects it leads people to believe in are not. We have spoken of the presupposition so far chiefly in terms of the contrast between 'What Percy says is true' and 'Things are as Percy says they are', which bear it, and 'For some p, both Percy says that p and p', which does not. The latter formula, (1), is for this reason inadequate. But it is not (1) which, by the end of Chapter 3, had been thought to provide an adequate analysis of 'What Percy says is true', but (25), of which '$\imath pJpp$' is the symbolic abbreviation. The difference between the comparatively simple (1) and the more complex (25), however, is irrelevant to the point we are making. Proposition (1) is of the form '$\Sigma pKSpp$', where 'S' is any operator forming a sentence out of a sentence. Now the two formulae '$\Sigma p\Pi qKEIpqJqp$' (which is simply the symbolic version of (25)) and '$\Sigma pK\Pi qEIpqJqp$', which differ only in that the order of 'Πq' and 'K' is reversed, are logically equivalent, and it is indeed only a matter of convention that (25) is written with the universal quantifier placed next to the existential at the beginning of the formula. Proposition (25) might very well have been written in the form symbolized by '$\Sigma pK\Pi qEIpqJqp$'. But this formula is itself of the form '$\Sigma pKSpp$'. '$\Pi qEIpqJq$' (which might well have been written '$\Pi qEJqIqp$', in which case we could have said simply that '$\Pi qEJqIq$' is substitutable for 'S') is a substitution instance of 'Sp'. So for practical purposes we may say that (25) as well as (1) is of the form '$\Sigma pKSpp$'. Now our point was this: propositions of the form '$\Sigma pKSpp$' entail corresponding propositions of the form 'ΣpSp'. But the relation between 'What Percy said is true' and 'Percy says something' is not one of entailment;

it is one of presupposition. 'Percy says something' is of the form '$\Sigma p S p$' and is entailed by (1). 'Percy says just one thing', i.e. '$\Sigma p \Pi q E I p q J q$', is also of the form '$\Sigma p S p$' and is similarly entailed by (25). The adjustment that needs to be made to (25) as an analysis of 'What Percy said is true' is one which makes '$\Sigma p \Pi q E I p q J q$' presupposed not entailed by the analysans. There is, of course, no symbolism at present to represent this. We could perhaps invent one. Using Frege's assertion sign '⊢' as a base, we might use a subscript to indicate that the sentence symbolized was one which made n assertions. The order of sentences following '$\vdash_n$' would indicate that the assertion of an earlier sentence was presupposed by the joint assertion of it and a later sentence. Using this symbolism, the symbolic analysis of 'What Percy says is true' would be

(30) $\vdash_2 \Sigma p \Pi q E I p q J q, \Pi r C J r r.$

But this symbolism does nothing more than crystallize what has already been said. It does not add anything.

It was a problem about the relation between 'What Percy says is true' and 'What Percy says is false' which led us to make the further refinements encapsulated in this formula. Like 'The King of France is bald' and 'The King of France is not bald' this pair of propositions seemed ill-fitted to being categorized either as contraries or as contradictories. 'What Percy says is false' can be represented in our newly invented symbolism by

(31) $\vdash_2 \Sigma p \Pi q E I p q J q, \Sigma r K J r N r.$

There is no name for the logical relation between (30) and (31). We shall not add to the impression of scholasticism by inventing one. The purpose of this consideration of falsehood has been, not so much to provide a new formalism for the analysis of truth, as to describe how the earlier and more *simpliste* formal analyses fall short of giving a complete account of the workings of our ordinary-language ascriptions of truth.

5
Correspondence

Aristotle's dictum that to say of what is that it is and of what is not that it is not (*vide supra*, pp. 67 seq.) has been regarded as the first statement of the Correspondence Theory of Truth.[1] There is, I believe, some justification for this. As we have seen, Aristotle's analysis, when suitably generalized, is tantamount to that propounded in this book. It is worthwhile asking in what sense this analysis is an analysis in terms of correspondence.

First we may look at some difficulties that correspondence theorists have run into. Our analysis may gain plausibility from the ways in which it makes it possible to meet these difficulties.

The view that the concept of truth involves the notion of correspondence seems to involve the view that truth is in some way relational. To say that something is true to say that it fits the facts, that it corresponds to what is the case; and *fitting* and *corresponding* seem to be relations. Not that truth can *be* a relation *tout court*. It is surprising to find Austin writing: 'we ask ourselves whether Truth is a substance (the Truth, the Body of Knowledge), or a quality (something like the colour red, inhering in truths) *or a relation* ("*correspondence*")';[2] and again 'if it is admitted (*if*) that the boring yet satisfactory relation between words and world which has here been discussed does genuinely occur, why should the phrase "is true" not be our way of describing it?'[3] Contrast Frege in 'The Thought': 'It might be supposed that truth consists in the correspondence of a picture with what it depicts. Correspondence is a relation. This is contradicted, however, by the use of the word "true", which is not a relation word and contains no reference to anything else to which something must correspond'.[4] A relation

---

[1] Cf. Körner, p. 101. Others have regarded this description of Aristotle's remark as misleading, cf. Ayer, p. 105.

[2] Austin, p. 111 (p. 18 in Pitcher): my italics.

[3] Austin, p. 128 (p. 31 in Pitcher).   [4] Frege, p. 18.

word is a two-place predicate. Since '— is true' is a one-place predicate it must stand not for a relation but for a property. But according to the Correspondence Theory the correct analysis of this one-place predicate is obtained by filling up one of the places of a two-place predicate. It may therefore be said to stand for a *relational* property. If it is like '— fits Freddie', which similarly is a one-place predicate obtained by filling up one of the places of a two-place predicate, '— is true' attributes to the statement whose name is attached to it a relation to some object other than itself. The difficulties Correspondence Theorists find themselves in are those of finding such an object and specifying the relation in which it stands to the statement said to be true.

If truth were a relational property of this sort, to say that something was true would be to say that it stood in a given relation to a given object, and to deny that it was true would be to deny that it stood in that relation to that object. If I deny the proposition 'This suit fits Freddie', the Freddie I say it doesn't fit is the same as the Freddie I would be saying it did fit if I were to affirm the proposition. If 'Toby sighed' is true it would, on this view, fit, or otherwise be related to, the fact that Toby sighed. But if 'Toby sighed' is false there is no such fact for it to fail to fit. A Correspondence Theory of Falsehood is more difficult to come by than a Correspondence Theory of Truth.

Russell at one[1] time held a view according to which if 'Toby sighed' is false, it and 'Toby did not sigh' both correspond to a single fact, the fact of Toby's not sighing. But this is not the sort of correspondence that, by itself at least, can explain the concept of truth. For on Russell's theory one can say that 'Toby sighed' corresponds to the fact that Toby didn't sigh, and whatever this does mean it certainly does not mean that 'Toby sighed' is true.

Even when it is true that Toby sighed there is some difficulty in finding an object *other than itself* for the statement to be related to. What is the fact which the proposition that Toby sighed, if true, fits? The fact, surely, that Toby sighed. The trouble here is that it fits too well. The *fitting* relation is interesting only if it is irreflexive.

[1] Russell (2), p. 187. I am grateful to Allen Long for drawing my attention to passages in Russell's writings which are relevant to my theme.

Information is not often to be gained from ascertaining that a structure is mappable on to itself. The fact that Toby sighed is not perhaps quite the same as the true proposition that Toby sighed, although this has been maintained. As Prior put it, 'facts and true propositions are alike "logical constructions", and...they are the same "logical constructions" (to have "true propositions" *and* "facts" is to have too *many* logical constructions)'.[1] But certainly the fact that Toby sighed looks uncannily like a projection on to reality of the proposition that Toby sighed. It would be odd, wouldn't it, to test whether the proposition that Toby sighed was true by taking the fact that Toby sighed and seeing whether the proposition fitted it?

This is the point at which Coherence Theorists hunting for something other than the true proposition itself for it to fit go whoring after strange propositions, propositions other than it.

The truth of 'Toby sighed' may consist in its fitting the fact that Toby sighed, but the truth of 'Toby died' cannot consist in this. There is no fact that every true proposition fits, although every true proposition fits some fact. If truth is a relational property of this sort the truth of each proposition must be a different relational property: '— is true' when attached to 'The proposition that Toby sighed' means '— fits the fact that Toby sighed', but when attached to 'The proposition that Toby died' means 'fits the fact that Toby died'. Some writers have made a virtue of this ambiguity:

> As philosophers, we tend to ask: What *makes* a proposition true? and in attempting to answer this question we tend to fly high into the realm of general forms of answer where we should keep to the rough ground of particular examples...If we want to know what makes propositions true then we must be prepared for as many different answers as there are propositions.   (Jones (1), p. 122.)

These difficulties which are involved in construing truth as a relational property arise also about *being married*.[2] To be married, one might say, is to stand in a relation to someone. Who then is the

---

[1] Prior (5), p. 5.

[2] Russell saw the analogy: 'The difference between a true and a false belief is like that between a wife and a spinster' (Russell (1), p. 165).

person to stand in a relation to whom is to be married? Who is the person to fail to stand in this relation to whom is to be unmarried? 'Someone' you reiterate. Yes, but who is it? The mistake you are making is that of taking 'someone' in '— is married to someone' as an argument of the function '— is married to...' A relational property, as we have been understanding the phrase, is signified by an expression obtained by attaching a name to a two-place predicate: '— is married to Henry VIII' signifies a relational property of this sort. But '— is married to someone' is obtained by attaching the first-level predicate '— is married to...' to the second-level predicate '...someone': the former is argument to the latter, not *vice versa*. This is seen by noticing that the contradictory of '— is married' is obtained by negating, not the relational expression '— is married to...', but the quantificational expression 'someone': ordinary language is slippery here, but one might risk the dictum that to be un-married is to be married to no one, not not to be married to someone.

The suggestion that is emerging is that '— is true' be analysed as something like

(32)   For some x, x is a fact and — corresponds to x,

just as '— is married' calls for the analysis

(33)   For some x, — is married to x.

The quest for the 'worldly' term of the correspondence relation is thus as futile as the quest for the 'someone' to whom a woman must be married if she is married. The fact that 'Toby sighed' fails to correspond to when it is false is like the 'someone' whom a woman fails to be married to if she is a spinster. The phenomenon we have here is in fact exactly the same as that which, on Russell's analysis at least, led Meinong to hunt for an object to correspond to expressions like 'The King of France'. On Russell's view sentences containing expressions of this sort should be analysed with the help of existential quantification. This would make the expression corresponding to 'is bald' in 'The King of France is bald' argument to the expression corresponding to 'The King of France', rather than *vice versa*,[1] just as we saw that '— is married to...' in '— is

---

[1] As we noted above, pp. 36 seqq., Russell's grasp of this truth sometimes slipped. It is Prior's reconstruction of Russell's symbolism which makes the point entirely clear.

married to someone' needs to be taken as argument to ' . . . someone', rather than *vice versa*.

The property of *being true*, then, demands analysis by some such
formula as (32), just as the property of *being married* demands
analysis by (33). Just as it would be a mistake to think that
what it meant to say of Jane Seymour that she was married
was to say that she was married to Henry VIII, so it is a
mistake to think that what it means to say of 'Toby sighed' that
it is true is to say that it corresponds to the fact that Toby sighed.[1]
So far we have been using the description 'relational property' only
for things like *being married to Henry VIII* or *corresponding to the
fact that Toby sighed*. Ought the properties which (32) and (33)
stand for also to be called relational? Surely *being married* is a
relational property?

The point is arguable. An analogous question is whether predicates like (32) are conjunctive predicates. If they are, one might
infer that propositions obtainable by attaching them to a subject-
expression were conjunctive propositions. This would lead to talk
of 'conjuncts' of such propositions. 'Something is a fact' might thus
be regarded as the conjunct of a proposition formed by attaching (32)
to a subject-expression, e.g. 'Something is a fact and Percy's statement corresponds to it'. But this would be a mistake. It would
tempt us to regard 'Percy's statement corresponds to it' as the other
conjunct, and thus as a complete proposition: and this would
probably lead to an erroneous account of the rôle of 'it' in this
sentence.[2] To prevent such mistakes it is advisable to limit the
description 'conjunctive' to those complex predicates in which
conjunction is the operation having the widest scope. (Polish
symbolism would allow instantaneous recognition of such predicates. The formal representation of a conjunctive predicate in this
symbolism would always have a 'K' at its extreme left.)

By analogy with this a complex predicate would be called relational
only if the relational expression in it were the operator having widest

[1] This is much the same mistake as the one Strawson is accused of on
p. 27 above.

[2] This point was touched on earlier, *vide supra*, pp. 25 seq. The importance
of the rôle of pronouns like 'it' in all this is well brought out by Geach in the
article cited in the footnote on p. 26.

scope. In '— is married to Henry VIII' Henry VIII is argument to
the function expressed by '— is married to...', and this is not in
its turn argument to any other function. In (33) on the other hand,
as has been pointed out, '— is married to ...' is argument to the
existential quantifier, which is thus the operator having widest scope
in the complex predicate. Such a predicate might more properly
be called quantificational than relational. Indeed the only way to
form a complex predicate that is relational in this strict sense is by
filling up argument places in a simple relational predicate with
genuine subject-expressions. A relational property thus understood
quite properly admits the question 'To what term does it relate
its possessor?' There was someone whose son one had to be if one
possessed the property of being a Tsarevich; it was the same person
whose son one had to fail to be if one lacked this property. To take
truth to be a relational property in this sense is to invite just those
questions about what it is that true propositions correspond to
which were found to be puzzling.

2

Clearly the Correspondence Theory must be rejected if it implies
that saying that something is true is saying that some relation holds
between it and an object. Of the two terms of this putative relation the
first, the Proposition, has been shown to be an illusion by the
reasoning of Chapter 3. The solution to the problem of the second
term of the relation had in fact already appeared in Chapter 2:
(17), like (32), is a quantificational predicate. However, (32), unlike
(17), contains what appears to be a relational expression '— corresponds to...'. In this it resembles (33). The argument of the
preceding paragraphs has brought out certain difficulties involved in
treating either (32) or (33) as standing for a relational property. But
surely there is *something* relational about being married? The relational expression '— is married to...' certainly enters into (33)
as an element in its composition, and if one likes to call a complex
predicate relational if a relational expression enters into it, and a
property relational if a complex predicate of this sort stands for it,
I suppose one may, as long as it is clear what is meant. There are
disadvantages in adopting this convention: complex predicates will

not now fall into mutually exclusive categories, 'conjunctive', 'relational', 'quantificational', etc. Expression (32), for example, will be describable in all these ways. The question 'Is (32) a quantificational or a relational predicate?' will be unanswerable.

Suppose, however, that we ignore these disadvantages and call *being married* a relational property on the grounds that a relational expression enters into its analysis. It appears that the same must be said about *truth*, since '— corresponds to . . .' occurs in (32). Truth may not be a relation, but can we deny that correspondence is? To be sure, Strawson, writing in 1950, was willing to deny this: 'The trouble with correspondence theories of truth . . . is the misrepresentation of " correspondence between statement and fact " as a relation, of any kind, between events or groups of things.'[1] But we can understand the two-place predicate '— corresponds to . . .' in expressions like (32), and relations just are what two-place predicates stand for. Perhaps Strawson's point is that correspondence is not a 'real' relation. What could be meant by this?

It might be claimed that the sense of the proposition formed by attaching (32) to, e.g., 'Percy's statement' is given by 'Things are as Percy says they are', and that this sentence contains no two-place predicate. The alleged relation of correspondence has thus been made to disappear under analysis. Just so we could make the ostensible three-term relation of *betweenness* disappear under analysis by pointing out that the proposition 'There was a disagreement between Austin and Strawson' could be paraphrased by 'Austin and Strawson disagreed with each other'.

The trouble with the analysis of 'Percy's statement corresponds with the facts' as 'Things are as Percy says they are' is that it is not clear whether it really is entitled to be called an analysis. Doubts about this have been expressed by G. J. Warnock.[2] He takes first a simpler analogue of 'Things are as Percy says they are', namely, 'He is as you have described'. There are some ways of speaking English in which 'He is like you have described' would be normal as a variant of 'He is as you have described'. 'Like' is a word which expresses a relation. If the possibility that the word 'like' can replace the word 'as' is taken as an indication of the meaning of the

---

[1] Strawson (2), p. 140 (p. 40 in Pitcher).   [2] Warnock, pp. 140 seqq.

latter, the sentence as a whole might be taken as expressing a relation between how the man in question is and how you have described him. It would be natural to describe this relation as that of *correspondence*.

Warnock does not commit himself to this line of argument. He has another way of reaching the same conclusion. Faced with the question 'What does it *mean* to say that he is as you have described?' he suggests the following explicatory paraphrase: 'The way that you have described him is the way he is'. This sentence does not *prima facie* express a relation: the first 'is' seems to be the 'is' of identity. But Warnock thinks this appearance deceptive. We have two definite descriptions, 'The way that you have described him' and 'the way he is' linked by the word 'is'; but what is asserted cannot, Warnock holds, be identity, because the one phrase 'really refers to a description, namely the description of him that you gave', while the other refers 'to his actual state, condition, character or what not'. Since the two phrases obviously, on Warnock's account, refer to different things, the statement as a whole cannot be asserting identity, but rather a relation between the things referred to. What can this relation be, other than *correspondence*?

Warnock is mistaken, however, in supposing that the phrases 'The way you have described him' and 'The way he is' refer to two different things. This is not to say that I believe them, in any clear sense, to 'refer' to one and the same thing. The language of *reference* is not helpful in cases like this, certainly not as a philosophical tool. Another way must be sought of reaching an understanding of propositions in which two definite descriptions are linked by 'is'.

Let us look first at the proposition 'The man Edith married is the man Alice married', where those who favour the language of reference would say that the definite descriptions referred, if the proposition was true, to one concrete spatio-temporal particular, more specifically, to a human being. What can certainly be said is that the proposition is true if one or other of the following propositions is true: 'Edith's sole hsuband was Harry and Alice's sole husband was Harry', 'Edith's sole husband was Arthur and Alice's sole husband was Arthur', 'Edith's sole husband was Fred and Alice's sole husband was Fred', . . . and so on. In all these cases we have a conjunctive proposition with a single name repeated in each of the conjuncts. It goes without saying that the name is taken to name the same man on each occurrence.

Warnock's proposition 'The way you have described him is the way he is' can be understood in a similar way. It is true if one or other of the following propositions is true. 'You have described him just as being fat and he is fat', 'You have described him just as being bad-tempered and he is bad-tempered', 'You have described him just as being a good batsman and he is a good batsman', ... and so on. (The word 'just' has to appear in these sentences, as the word 'sole' had to appear in the earlier set, to take care of the uniqueness implied by 'the' in 'the way you have described him'.) In all these cases we have a conjunctive proposition with a single predicative expression repeated in each of the conjuncts.

In our attempt in Chapter 1 to understand the analysis of 'What Percy says is true' provided by (1), we remarked that (1) is understood if we realize that (1) is true when replacing 'p' by a sentence in that part of (1) which follows the phrase 'For some p,', yields a true proposition: (1) is true if 'Percy says that Mabel has measles and Mabel has measles' is true. This can be generalized for all existentially quantified formulae. Any proposition of the form 'For some θ, ... θ ...' is true if replacing 'θ' by an appropriate constant in '... θ ...' yields a true proposition. It is clear, therefore, that the same propositions whose truth will, as we have seen, verify the truth of 'The man Edith married is the man Alice married' will also verify the truth of

(34)   For some x, Edith's sole husband was x and Alice's sole husband was x,

where the constants corresponding to the variable 'x' are names like 'Harry', 'Arthur' or 'Fred'. Similarly, the same propositions whose truth will verify 'The way you have described him is the way he is' will also verify the truth of

(35)   For some F, you described him just as being F and he is F,

where the constants corresponding to the variable 'F' are predicative expressions like 'fat', 'bad-tempered' or 'a good batsman'. If 'The man Edith married is the man Alice married' is describable as an identity proposition 'The way you have described him is the way he is' may also be described as an identity proposition. At all events the former can hardly be described as asserting a relation between two distinct men. Neither can the latter be described as asserting a relation between a description and a man's 'actual state'.

(Warnock's claim that 'The way you have described him' refers to a description can be countered by the following considerations: Just as 'The man Edith married' is rendered by logicians as 'The x such that Edith married x', 'The way you have described him' might be rendered as 'The F such that you have described him as being F'. The first of these phrases would not be taken by those who talk of 'referring expressions' as referring to a name: if it refers to anything it refers to a man. The second phrase, by parity of reasoning, should not be said to 'refer' to a description: if it refers to anything it refers to the 'actual state, condition, character or what not' of the person described.)

Warnock extends the considerations he brings forward about the proposition 'The way you have described him is the way he is' to the proposition 'The statement that p represents things in a certain way which is the way things are'. The two items which the words '*which is*' ostensibly identify are, according to Warnock, 'on the one hand, a certain propositional representation of the way things are, and on the other hand the way things are'. Since these two items are plainly distinct the proposition in question cannot be supposed really to be asserting their identity: it must rather be taken as asserting a relation between them, and this relation would most naturally be called 'correspondence'.

One may remark that on a literal reading of Warnock's proposition it is not the representation offered by the statement that p which is the antecedent of 'which' in the phrase 'which is the way things are' but *the way in which* the statement that p represents things. This 'way' is no more a 'propositional representation' than the 'way you described him' is a description. The phrase 'the way in which the statement that p represents things' might be rendered in logicians' jargon as 'the q such that the statement that p states that q'. If we avoid unnecessarily multiplying variables by replacing Warnock's phrase 'the statement that p' by our own 'What Percy says' or 'Percy's statement', we can render this as 'the q such that Percy's statement states that q'. 'The way things are' analogously comes out as 'The r such that r'.[1] What the Warnockian version of 'Percy's statement is true' reduces to is, therefore, 'The q such that Percy's statement states that q is identical with the r such that r'.

Once again, this has an analogy in terms of Edith and Alice. 'The y such that Edith married y is identical with the z such that Alice married z' is true if, for example, Edith's sole husband was Harry and Alice's sole husband was Harry, or if Edith's sole husband was Arthur and Alice's sole husband was Arthur,..., and so on. Similarly 'The q such that Percy's statement states that q is identical with the r such that r' is true if, for example, Percy's statement states that there is raging inflation and there is raging inflation, or if Percy's statement states that Big Ben is striking and Big Ben is striking, or..., and so on. Again, as we have seen, 'The man Edith married is the man Alice married' works in the same way as (34). Analogously we can see that the Warnockian 'Percy's statement represents things in a certain way which is the way things are' works in the same way as (18) 'For some p, both Percy's statement states that p and p'.

It was felt as a difficulty that 'Things are as Percy says they are' and similar paraphrases of 'Percy's statement is true' do not obviously provide 'analyses' of the notion of truth. Warnock complained that such paraphrases themselves pose problems of interpretation, particularly in respect of the part played in them by the word 'as', and his own attempt at interpreting them has recourse to the notion of *correspondence*, seen as a relation between what is said and what is the case. The trouble with this notion is that it is at least as obscure as the notion of *truth* itself, and cannot confidently be employed as part of an analysis of that notion.

It appears, however, that the belief that *correspondence* has to be introduced into an explication of 'Things as are Percy says they are', or the analogous 'He is as you have described him', is mistaken. These propositions can themselves most easily be construed as

---

[1] Taken out of context, of course, this is nonsense. There is no *one* r such that r. But the same considerations apply to 'the way things are'.

having the forms displayed in (18) and (35), forms which themselves explain the rôle played by the word 'as' in these propositions.
That is to say, they have a structure similar to that displayed by the
logicians' devices of conjunction and quantification with its attendant
variables. To the extent that the ordinary language proposition
'Things are as Percy says they are' shares the structure of (18) it
can quite properly be said to provide an analysis of 'What Percy
says is true'. What has been achieved in this case is the explanation
of the concept of truth in terms merely of quantification and conjunction. Quine claimed that the whole conceptual apparatus of
mathematics could be reduced by a series of definitions to three undefined notions: quantification, the primitive truth-function and
class membership.[1] Similarly quantification, identity and truth-
functions are by themselves, I maintain, sufficient to define the
notion of truth. In (25) and (30) they do that part of the work done
in 'What Percy says is true' by the words 'What...is true'. The
words 'Percy says' remain in the analysis exactly as they were in
the proposition analysed. (Only the word 'that' is new, and it is
logically insignificant and eliminable.)

Whether or not Quine succeeds in the task he sets himself in
Mathematical Logic, we can surely agree that *if* he succeeds the
definitions or paraphrases he provides constitute a genuine 'analysis'
of the complex notions that constitute his *definienda*. In the same
way, it can hardly be disputed that Frege provides us with an
'analysis' of the proposition 'There are the same number of *F*s as
there are *G*s' by paraphrasing this in terminology that does not go
beyond first-order logic and identity. This enterprise of 'analysis'
is in the same tradition as Euclid's *Elements* with its reduction by
definition of the vocabulary of geometry to a few undefined terms.
So it should not be complained of a definition of truth in terms
simply of 'some', 'the same' and 'and' that it fails to achieve an
'analysis' in this *genre*.

3

It is possible, then, without circularity to find a paraphrase of 'For
some x, x is a fact and Percy's statement corresponds to x' which

[1] Cf. Quine (1), p. 126.

does not contain a two-place predicate. Proposition (18) does contain one expression '— states that . . .' which at first sight might be mistaken for a two-place predicate. But this expression is, in Timothy Potts's terminology, a 'relator'. It is a predicate, at best, 'only at one end' (*vide supra* p. 56), the end which can be completed by such subject-expressions as 'Percy's statement'. Even if this term of the apparent relation were to survive, since the other term has failed to survive our analysis, the claim of correspondence to involve a genuine relation could not be made good. A relation has to have two terms.

In fact, as is already clear, neither term survives a thorough examination. 'Percy's statement states that p' is at first sight nothing more than a blown-up version of 'Percy states that p'. Perhaps some implication of uniqueness is involved in the use of 'Percy's statement states' rather than 'Percy states': Percy might state that p *amongst other things*, but there can only be one thing that Percy's statement states. To take account of this, however, we need only employ the techniques used in Chapter 3 to represent the uniqueness of 'What Percy says'. To the extent that (25) represents 'What Percy says is true' it will also represent (18). To the extent that (25) needs revision to take account of the fact that the use of the phrase 'Percy's statement', like that of 'What Percy says', presupposes rather than entails that Percy says just one thing, the refinements introduced into the analysis in Chapter 4 will take care of this. More complicated phrases occupying the subject position in front of the 'relator' will succumb to more complicated treatment. 'That notice states that p' can be regarded as shorthand for 'If anyone were to utter assertively the words written on that notice he would be asserting that p'. 'Utilitarianism states that p' will perhaps be rendered 'Anyone who is a Utilitarian holds that p'. In general it is always possible to substitute for a phrase in which a sentence, 'p', is linked to an apparent designation of an abstract propositional object by the words 'states that', another phrase in which 'p' is linked by this or some other 'relator' to the name, not of an abstract object, but of a person, or to a variable whose range is the class of persons.

To return to the alleged correspondence relation: both of its terms have been eliminated in favour of expressions involving the existential quantifier. Indeed *the same* quantifier serves, with the variables it binds, to do the work done by the expressions standing for the terms of the correspondence relation in, say, 'Percy's statement corresponds with the facts'. 'Percy's statement' disappears in the analysis in favour of the existential quantifier with the variable '*p*' and the open sentence 'Percy says that *p*', or whatever more elaborate open sentence needs to be devised along the lines of (25). 'The facts' disappears in favour of the same 'For some *p*,' together this time with the minimal open sentence '*p*'. Nor is any word or phrase left to correspond with correspondence except, perhaps, the words 'both...and'. Certainly there is no trace anywhere in this analysis of a two-place predicate.

We saw that truth could not be categorized as a relational property in the sense that a complex predicate stood for it in which the operator having the widest scope was a relational expression. But being married would not qualify as a relational property by this criterion, and yet there seemed to be *something* relational about being married. This could be accounted for in that the complex predicate (33) which signified *being married* contained a genuine relational expression '— is married to...'. But the relational expression '— corresponds to...' occurring in the complex predicate (32), which was serving as a provisional analysis of '— is true', seemed not to be genuine in this sense. When the analysis was taken further neither it nor any two-place predicate at all played any rôle in the elucidatory paraphrase arrived at. It seems that *truth* cannot be called a relational property even in the less exacting sense in which *being married* can be so called.

4

And yet there does seem to be *something* relational about truth. Warnock attempted to elucidate this feeling along the following lines:

> I should take the unperspicuous but widely shared notion that 'truth is relational' to be a way of giving expression to the profoundly uncontroversial thought that the question whether a proposition (let us say – but 'belief', or 'statement', or 'assertion' would do just as well here) is or is not true is not in general to be

determined by mere consideration of what that proposition is,
of the proposition itself or of what it 'states'. If you tell me that
there are badgers at the bottom of your garden, I may well be
absolutely clear as to what it is that you have said; your proposition may be set plainly before me, in all its aspects; I may know
exactly what statement you have made, what belief you have
expressed. But – the thought is – I do not thereby know, nor
am I thereby in a position to determine, whether it (the proposition, etc.) is true or false. Whether it is true or false turns on,
and the determination of that question calls for reference to,
something else; I shall not get anywhere merely by musing on
what the proposition is, since it could, of course, be precisely
that proposition, and nevertheless be either a true proposition,
or a false one. What practically everybody agrees on is, one
might say, that the truth or falsehood of propositions is determined by *something* 'outside' the propositions themselves; a
false proposition is not necessarily a different proposition from
the proposition it would have been had it been true, or vice-
versa. That truth is a 'relational property' seems a natural way
enough of expressing this; for perhaps one thing that a relational
property is, is a property such that an item may either possess or
lack it without thereby being itself different.

(Warnock, pp. 136 seq.)

One thing that Warnock is claiming here seems to be plainly wrong.
A property is not *ipso facto* a relational property if the mere knowledge of what the object is to which it is being ascribed is insufficient
to determine whether the object possesses that property or not. On
such an interpretation of 'relational property' baldness would be
a relational property. Substituting 'the Bishop of Bristol' for 'there
are badgers at the bottom of your garden' one might argue by
parity of reasoning as follows: 'If you speak to me of the Bishop of
Bristol I may well be absolutely clear as to who it is that you have
mentioned; the person you refer to may be set plainly before me,
in all his aspects. I may know exactly whom you have spoken of,
which person you have indicated. But...I do not thereby know
whether he is bald or has a good head of hair'. It may be objected

that if His Lordship is 'set plainly before me' I shall be in a position to know if he is bald. But perhaps he has his mitre on. — Yes, but the proposition is said to be set plainly before me *in all its aspects*. Is not truth, then, one of its aspects?

Whatever we make of things' being 'set plainly before us in all their aspects', particularly when the objects in question are such mysterious entities as Propositions (or statements, or beliefs, or assertions), it seems clear that Warnock is here confusing a property's being relational with its being contingent. Just as the identification of the Bishop of Bristol has nothing to do with his being, or not being, bald, so the identification of a Proposition is in general entirely independent of its truth-value. With the notable exception of analytic Propositions, truth and falsehood are not necessary properties of Propositions any more than baldness, as opposed to maleness – or being human, to avoid the point being too rapidly overtaken by ecclesiastical change – is of bishops.

Maybe Warnock's remarks about the identification of the subject of the property should be discounted, and what we should attend to is his metaphorical use of the word 'outside'. In order to determine whether the Bishop of Bristol is bald we do not have to pay attention to anything outside the Bishop – let us assume for the moment that the Bishop's hair, if he has any, is part of him. To determine, on the other hand, whether the Bishop is taller than the Dean we have to pay attention to something outside him, to the Dean in fact. Warnock's summarizing comment suggests that he is the victim of some ambiguity here: he says 'perhaps one thing that a relational property is, is a property such that an item may either possess it or lack it without thereby being itself different'. If the difference in question is the opposite of *specific* identity, the view that being taller than the Dean is a relational property may be suitably expressed by saying that the Bishop may possess it or lack it without thereby himself being different. His baldness could not so be described. But if the difference in question is the opposite of *numerical* identity – as Warnock's remarks about knowing 'exactly what statement you have made', etc., suggest – then the Bishop could possess or lack baldness too without thereby being himself different; he would still be the same man.

The difficulty here is that Propositions cannot be said literally to have things 'outside' them. They are not objects we inspect, as we may inspect bishops to see if they are bald. The only thing that could be contrasted with looking 'outside' the Proposition is determining the identity of the Proposition. What Percy says is identified by establishing what words Percy utters, what those words mean and what is the context of their utterance. Propositions, being logical constructions, can have very few 'intrinsic' properties. A logical construction is always less hospitable to properties than a material object; the average Bristol 'bus conductor can be exactly 5 ft. 10 in. tall, but he cannot be engaged to the Bishop's grand-daughter. So it may well be that in the case of Propositions proper-ties necessary for identity and intrinsic properties coincide. Whether what Percy says is true is not determined, unless its truth is analytic, merely by discovering what Percy says. But the only thing that can be discovered by examining what Percy says *itself* is what it is that Percy says. To find out anything else about what Percy says we have to look elsewhere.

In particular, if what Percy says is that Mabel has measles, to find out whether what Percy says is true we have to examine Mabel, or listen to someone who has examined her. This much may be conceded to those who insist on the relational character of truth. Explications of ascriptions of truth come in two bits:

> What the policeman said was true.
>
> What do you mean?
>
> Well, the policeman said that the door was unlocked and the door *was* unlocked.

To find out whether what Percy says is true we have to find out what it is that Percy says and, having found this out, to find out whether Mabel has measles. The 'verifier' of 'What Percy says is true' will be a conjunctive proposition: one conjunct will tell us what Percy says, the other will in general have nothing at all to do with Percy.

Expression (33), the *analysans* of '— is married', was, in a broad sense, relational because it contained a two-place predicate, albeit this was not the expression having widest scope in (33). Expression (17) was not relational even in this sense because it contained no

two-place predicate at all. But (17) contains the word 'and', and
'— is married...' and '— and...' have this at least in common:
both are functions of two arguments. Truth-functions are not
relations: Quine often insists on our distinguishing the relation
expressed by 'implies' from the logical connective expressed by
'If — then...' But there is an isomorphism between logical connectives and relations, which we take note of by calling them both
functions of two arguments. The mistake which Quine warns us
against is a natural one. It is easy to suppose that 'If p then q' states
a relation between 'p' and 'q'. Similarly, when faced with a conjunctive verifier of a statement ascribing truth, we may smell something
relational in the concept of truth itself: 'Mary said that John was out
and John *was* out. So what she said was true. It corresponded with
the facts. Things were as she said they were.' Or, to adopt the
variant already mentioned (*vide supra*, p. 80), 'Things were *like* she
said they were'. 'As' is a conjunction, 'like' a preposition. Preposi-
tions are used to express relations, conjunctions are sentential connectives. But we are not always very good at remembering the
distinction. Fowler would shudder at 'Things were like she said they
were', but many would find it as natural as 'Mary is like John'. If the
ordinary vernacular permits use of a relational word, 'like', in an
ordinary-language equivalent of 'What she said was true', philosophers may be forgiven for diagnosing a concept as relational, when all
that was really in evidence was the less specific phenomenon, a function of two arguments.

5

Nevertheless, it may well be doubted whether the mere presence of
conjunction in a paraphrase of '— is true' is enough to explain the
readiness with which philosophers accept the idea that there is
something relational about the concept of truth. J. L. Mackie is committed to a theory of truth which is substantially the same as that put
forward in this book.[1] He rejects, as we have done (*vide supra*,
pp. 26 seqq.), the view that 'to say that the-statement-that-p is true
is to say that, as the statement states, p... It equates' he says 'saying
that the-statement-that-p is true with the conjunction of two items'.[2]

---

[1] Cf. Mackie (1) and his discussion of the topic in Mackie (2).
[2] Mackie (1), p. 328.

According to him these two items are 'p' and 'this is as the statement states'. This is unfortunate, because the second of these items (where 'this' is, surely, a pronoun of laziness) is identical with the original 'As the statement states, p' which the conjunction was supposed to represent. It cannot be right to identify a conjunction with one of its conjuncts. Mackie is not quite right, however, in analysing 'As the statement states, p' as a simple conjunction. It was my preliminary view (*vide supra*, pp. 20 seq.) that this was so, although the conjuncts were there given as 'p' and 'the statement states that p'. The findings of Chapter 4, however, (*vide supra*, pp. 63 seq., 68 seq.) imply that to assert 'As the statement states, p' is not to assert a conjunctive proposition but jointly to assert two propositions. But whether or not the conjunction of these propositions is asserted, Mackie is wrong to say that the propositions in question give us 'an element of reassertion' and 'an element of comparison'. If the second proposition is replaced, as it must be, by 'The statement states that p', it becomes obvious that no 'element of comparison' is involved. So 'As the-statement-that-p states, p' is in fact even less well equipped than Mackie believes it is for providing an analysis of 'The-statement-that-p is true'. It is not even partially a 'comparison account'; and, as Mackie sees, it is the element of comparison that is 'vital for the ascription of truth'. Comparison is provided only by what Mackie calls the 'pure comparison account', which gives 'Things are as the-statement-that-p states' as the analysis of 'The-statement-that-p is true'. This account, he says, 'locates truth in a certain relation'.[1]

We have seen reason to doubt whether 'this account' does entitle us to speak of truth as a relational concept. It produces a paraphrase of '— is true' which lacks any two-place predicate and it makes the apparent terms of the correspondence relation disappear. They disappear, as has been remarked (*vide supra*, pp. 86 seq.), in favour of two open sentences whose variables are bound by a single quantifier. Bound variables, as is well recognized, do much of the work done in ordinary discourse by the relative pronouns 'who', 'which', etc. It has been claimed earlier (*vide supra*, pp. 19 seqq.) that sentential variables bound by a quantifier do much of the work

[1] *Ibid.*, p. 329.

done in the vernacular by the conjunction 'as'. The analogy between 'as' and 'who', 'which' etc. has been drawn out by speaking of 'as' not as a conjunction but as a relative adverb – or perhaps relative pro-adverb. *Relative* pronouns are so called, I suppose, because they *refer* back to their antecedents. This cross-*reference* is precisely the function of the variables of quantification, and this applies to sentential as well as to individual variables, when quantification of these occurs. The etymological connection between 'relative', 'reference' and 'relation' ought not to be overlooked.

The expression formed by the existential quantifier and an *individual* variable and two bound *individual* variables each of which occurs in an open sentence forming one conjunct of a conjunctive matrix may be regarded as signifying a second-level relation. 'For some x, both — x and $...x$' yields a complete sentence when two first-level predicates are inserted in its gaps. For instance (34) is formed by attaching to this second-level predicate the two first-level predicates 'Edith's sole husband was —' and 'Alice's sole husband was —'. Frege would have described (34) as asserting that a second-level relation held between these two first-level concepts. One can even say what the relation is: it is the relation that holds between two concepts when a single object falls under them both.

The relation that is *said* to hold between two concepts by (34) is perhaps *shown* to hold between them by any of the 'verifiers' of (34), e.g. 'Edith's sole husband was Harry and Alice's sole husband was Harry'. Or, since a 'verifier' entails the proposition it verifies, we might more accurately state the case thus: *part* of what is said by a 'verifier' of (34) will be that this relation holds between the two concepts.

Unlike (34), (18) does not split up into a second-level predicate and two first-level predicates. However, (18) like (34) involves an existential quantifier binding two variables; but they are sentential, not individual variables. This being so, the second of these variables is capable of forming a complete open sentence by itself, and leaves no gap to be filled by an expression of any category. Prior[1] utilized the words 'verb' and 'adverb' to classify in syntactical categories expressions which play a part in our sentences. Taking 'name'

[1] Prior (3), pp. 6 seqq.

and 'sentence' as primitive, undefined terms, he defined 'verbs' as expressions which form sentences out of names and 'adverbs' as expressions that form sentences out of sentences. Thus as well as 'Possibly' and 'Necessarily', which are adverbs by standard grammatical criteria, truth-functions and expressions like 'Charles believes that' and 'Percy says that' are adverbs in Prior's sense. 'For some x, both — x and . . .x' might, by an extension of Prior's terminology, be called a second-level verb, since it forms a sentence out of what Prior would count as verbs. The partial[1] analysis of 'What Percy says is false' as equivalent to 'For some p, both Percy says that p and it is not the case that p' might analogously be said to involve a second-level adverb: 'For some p, both — p and . . .p' is here made into a complete sentence by its gaps' being filled by the two 'adverbs' 'Percy says that' and 'it is not the case that'. This second-level adverb and the two first-level adverbs that are its arguments form a structure which is isomorphic with that formed by the second-level verb and the two first-level verbs which are its arguments in (34). Proposition (34) could be said to state a relation between concepts. But there is no safe 'material mode' way of describing what is stated by 'For some p, both Percy says that p and it is not the case that p': it would be misleading in far too many ways to say that it expressed a relation between *being said by Percy* and *not being the case*.

Still less can we pick out a relation whose existence is clearly stated by (1), or its variants. 'For some p, both — p and . . .p' is a second-level adverb which can be made into a complete sentence by filling its gaps with 'adverbs' or by filling one of its gaps with an adverb and closing the other gap up, or by closing both gaps up. This last procedure, which would yield 'For some p, both p and p', is uninteresting. The formula thus produced is equivalent to 'For some p, p' ('Something or other is the case'), and is if anything still less likely to be asserted by anyone. But filling up the first gap in our second-level adverb with 'Percy says that' and closing the other gap up yields our original paraphrase of 'What Percy says is true'. We will not at this stage of the argument be surprised to find that we have on our hands a formula which can stand either as a complete sentence or as the expression of a function which yields

---

[1] Partial, because it takes no account of the uniqueness of what Percy says.

a complete sentence by the insertion of one or more expressions into it. The expression '$\imath pJpp$' is a second-level adverb of this sort, and we discussed at length in Chapter 3 its capacity for receiving an 'adverbial' addition between its two last variables. We also showed how this was an inevitable consequence of allowing sentential variables to be bound by quantifiers. The phenomenon we are at present examining is the same. But it is not one we should readily describe as 'relational'.

Nevertheless, we can trace a series of analogies from (1) to straightforwardly relational sentences, which goes some way to explaining why philosophers have wanted to say that there is something relational about truth. 'Mary is behind John' is a sentence composed of two names and a first-level two-place predicate. It clearly states a relation between two human beings. 'For some x, Edith's sole husband was x and Alice's sole husband was x', (34), is a sentence composed of two first-level one-place predicates and a second-level two-place predicate. It can be said to state a relation between two concepts. 'For some p, both Percy says that p and it is not the case that p' is a sentence composed of two first-level one-place 'adverbs' and one second-level two-place 'adverb'. This proposition cannot safely be said to state a relation between any two items, but its similarity with (34) is obvious. It is similar also to (1) in that the same second-level adverb enters into (1), although on this occurrence it expresses a function of only one argument. (The same expression could appear as a complete sentence, i.e. not as an adverb at all.) These overlapping similarities explain, even if they do not justify, the feeling that truth is a relational concept.

We can even allow that there is something relational, 'an element of comparison', in 'verifiers' of (1) like 'Percy says that Mabel has measles and Mabel has measles'. Such propositions are indeed conjunctive propositions in the strict sense – conjunction is the operation having widest scope in the proposition – but they are conjunctive propositions with a distinctive feature. Their merely being conjunctive propositions is not enough to account for the feeling that they are relational, and it is certainly a mistake to identify one of their conjuncts with an 'element of comparison' (*vide supra*, pp. 91 seq.). But the repetition in the second conjunct of an element which occurred in the first binds the parts of the proposition together rather more tightly than mere conjunction could do. As we have seen (*vide supra*, pp. 21 seqq.) such propositions can be described as asserting something of an object or person mentioned in only one conjunct: 'A's statement states that X is eligible and X is eligible' genuinely asserts something of A's statement. Again, we can understand the urge to say that such a proposition shows, if it does not say, that a relation holds between A's statement and reality. Since it entails the proposition 'For some *p*, both A's statement states that *p* and *p*', this can indeed be regarded as part of what it says, and the reasons for wanting to call *this* relational have already been spelled out.

The relation between A's statement and reality just referred to is the relation of correspondence. To say that things are as Percy says they are is, of course, to say that Percy's statement corresponds to the facts. There is nothing wrong with the Correspondence Theory if it limits itself to pointing out that 'What Percy says is true' means the same as 'What Percy says corresponds to the facts'. So much is evident to anyone who knows how to speak English. What is questionable is whether so far we have a 'theory'. The relation of correspondence is at least as problematic as the concept of truth. Is the notion of correspondence something that has to be brought in, as Warnock thinks, to explain the meaning of 'as' in 'Things are as Percy says they are', or does the latter explain the notion of correspondence? The second alternative is the one adopted in this book. Not that matters are left there. 'Things are as Percy says they are' is itself something whose meaning can be elucidated with the help of quantification, identity, truth-functions and sentential variables. The apparatus does not include anything explicitly relational, but the analogies which exist between the sentences we are enabled by its means to construct and sentences which can properly be called relational are sufficient to make talk of a relation of correspondence understandable and natural. There is nothing more to be done. It is profitless mystification to talk of a relation which (1) or (25) or (30) does not say exists, but shows to exist. We are not here in the realms of the unsayable. 'What Percy says is true' can be said, and the clearest way of saying it is by way of the analyses we have given. Truth is as simple as that.

Appendix

List of inset, numbered expressions discussed in the text

(1) For some p, both Percy says that p and p

(2) For some p, both Percy says that p and it is true that p

(3) For some x, both x is old and x is tired

(4) For some p, p

(5) Edith married a man *whom* Alice married

(6) Edith married some man *and* Alice married *him*

(7) Edith married Harry, *who* was a butcher

(8) Edith married Harry, *and he* was a butcher

(9) A's statement states that X is eligible and X is eligible

(10) John married Susan and Susan is Mary's daughter

(11) Susan's hat is shocking pink and Mary's hat is shocking pink

(12) Lord Justice Halsbury holds there was negligence and Lord Justice Salisbury holds there was negligence

(13) For some x, both — married x and x is Mary's daughter

(14) For some F, both — is F and Mary's hat is F

(15) For some p, both — holds that p and Lord Justice Salisbury holds that p

(16) For some p, both A's statement states that p and p

(17) For some p, both — states that p and p

(18) For some p, both Percy's statement states that p and p

(19) What the postman brought is on the mantelpiece

(20) For some x, for every y, both x is the same thing as y if, and only if, the postman brought y and x is on the mantelpiece

(21) What the postman brought

(22) For some x, for every y, both x is the same thing as y if, and only if, the post man brought y and

(23) For some x, for every y, both x is the same thing as y if, and only if, the postman brought y and x

(24) For some x, for every y, both x is the same thing as y if, and only if, the postman brought y and Henry thinks that x is on the mantelpiece

(25) For some p, for every q, both the proposition that p is the same proposition as the proposition that q if, and only if, Percy says that q and p

(26) For some p, for every q, both the proposition that p is the same proposition as the proposition that q if, and only if, Percy says that q and

(27) Percy says that grass is red and it is not the case that grass is red

(28) Simon was brought by the postman, and nothing else was brought by the postman, and Simon is on the mantelpiece

(29) Percy says that Mabel has measles, and Percy says nothing else, and Mabel has measles

(30) $\vdash_2 \Sigma p \Pi q E I p q J q, \Pi r C J r r$

(31) $\vdash_2 \Sigma p \Pi q E I p q J q, \Sigma r K J r N r$

(32) For some x, x is a fact and — corresponds to x

(33) For some x, — is married to x

(34) For some x, Edith's sole husband was x and Alice's sole husband was x

(35) For some F, you described him just as being F and he is F

Bibliography

Aristotle, *Metaphysics*, ed. W. D. Ross, Oxford: At the Clarendon Press, 1924.

Austin, J. L., 'Truth' in *Proceedings of the Aristotelian Society*, supplementary vol. 24, 1950, reprinted in J. L. Austin, *Philosophical Papers*, Oxford: Oxford University Press, 1970, and in Pitcher, *vide infra*.

Ayer, A. J., *Russell and Moore: the Analytical Heritage*, London: Macmillan, 1971.

Cohen, L. J., (1) Review of Prior (5) in *Mind*, vol. 82, 1973.

    (2) 'Roger Gallie on Substitutional Quantification' in *Analysis*, vol. 34, no. 3, 1974.

Dummett, Michael, *Frege: Philosophy of Language*, London: Duckworth, 1973.

Frege, Gottlob, 'The Thought' in P. F. Strawson (ed.) *Philosophical Logic*, Oxford: Oxford University Press, 1967.

Gallie, R. D., (1) 'A. N. Prior and Substitutional Quantification' in *Analysis*, vol. 34, no. 3, 1974.

    (2) 'Substitutionalism and Substitutional Quantification' in *Analysis*, vol. 35, no. 3, 1975.

Geach, P. T., (1) 'Russell's Theory of Descriptions' in *Analysis*, vol. 10, no. 4, 1950, reprinted in Margaret Macdonald (ed.), *Philosophy and Analysis*, Oxford: Basil Blackwell, 1954.

    (2) 'Ascriptivism' in *The Philosophical Review*, vol. 69, 1960, reprinted in Geach (6).

    (3) *Reference and Generality*, Ithaca: Cornell University Press, 1962.

    (4) 'Assertion' in *The Philosophical Review*, vol. 74, 1965, reprinted in Geach (6).

    (5) 'Logical Procedures and the Identity of Expressions' in *Ratio*, vol. 7, 1965, reprinted in Geach (6).

    (6) *Logic Matters*, Oxford: Basil Blackwell, 1972.

Grover, Dorothy L., Camp, Joseph L., Jr, and Belnap, Nuel D., Jr, 'A Prosentential Theory of Truth' in *Philosophical Studies*, vol. 27, 1975.

Jones, O. R., (1) 'In Disputation of an Undisputed Thesis' in *Analysis*, vol. 28, no. 4, 1968.

    (2) 'On Truth – a Reply to C. J. F. Williams' in *Analysis*, vol. 31, no. 1, 1970.

    (3) 'Truth and Predication' in *Analysis*, vol. 32, no. 3, 1972.

Kirwan, Christopher (ed.), *Metaphysics ΓΔE*, Oxford: At the Clarendon Press, 1971.

Kneale, William, 'Propositions and Truth in Natural Languages' in *Mind*, vol. 81, 1972.

Kneale, William and Martha, *The Development of Logic*, Oxford: At the Clarendon Press, 1962.

Körner, Stephan, *What is Philosophy?* London: Allen Lane, The Penguin Press, 1969.

Mackie, J. L., (1) 'Simple Truth' in *The Philosophical Quarterly*, vol. 20, 1970.
    (2) *Truth, Probability, and Paradox*, Oxford: At the Clarendon Press, 1972.

Pitcher, George (ed.), *Truth*, Englewood Cliffs, New Jersey: Prentice-Hall Inc., 1964.

Prior, A. N., (1) 'Is the Concept of Referential Opacity Really Necessary?' in *Acta Philosophica Fennica*, vol. 16, 1963.
    (2) 'On Spurious Egocentricity' in *Philosophy*, vol. 42, 1967, reprinted in Prior (3).
    (3) *Papers on Time and Tense*, Oxford: At the Clarendon Press, 1968.
    (4) 'Intensionality and Intentionality' in *Proceedings of the Aristotelian Society*, supplementary vol. 42, 1968.
    (5) *Objects of Thought*, Oxford: At the Clarendon Press, 1971.

Quine, W. V., (1) *Mathematical Logic*, New York: Harper Torchbooks, 1962.
    (2) *From a Logical Point of View*, New York: Harper Torchbooks, 1963.
    (3) *Word and Object*, Cambridge, Massachusetts: The M.I.T. Press, 1967.
    (4) *Ontological Relativity and Other Essays*, New York: Columbia University Press, 1969.

Ramsey, F. P., *The Foundations of Mathematics*, Totowa, New Jersey: Littlefield, Adams and Co., 1965.

Russell, Bertrand, (1) *Human Knowledge, its Scope and Limits*, London: Allen and Unwin, 1948.
    (2) *Logic and Knowledge*, ed. R. C. Marsh, London: Allen and Unwin, 1956.

Ryle, Gilbert, 'Plato's "Parmenides"' in *Mind*, vol. 48, 1939, reprinted in R. E. Allen (ed.), *Studies in Plato's Metaphysics*, London: Routledge and Kegan Paul, 1965.

Sayward, Charles, (1) 'Williams' Definition of "*X* is True"' in *Analysis*, vol. 30, no. 3, 1970.
    (2) 'True Propositions: a Reply to C.J. F. Williams' in *Analysis*, vol. 32, no. 3, 1972.

Strawson, P. F., (1) 'Truth' in *Analysis*, vol. 9, no. 6, 1949, reprinted in Margaret Macdonald (ed.), *Philosophy and Analysis*, Oxford: Basil Blackwell, 1954.
    (2) 'Truth' in *Proceedings of the Aristotelian Society*, supplementary vol. 24, 1950, reprinted in Pitcher, *vide supra*.
    (3) *Individuals: an Essay in Descriptive Metaphysics*, London: Methuen, 1959.
    (4) 'A Problem about Truth: a Reply to Mr. Warnock' in Pitcher, *vide supra*.

Warnock, G. J., 'Truth: or Bristol Revisited' in *Proceedings of the Aristotelian Society*, supplementary vol. 47, 1973.

White, A. R., *Truth*, New York: Anchor Books, 1970.

Whitehead, A. N. and Russell, Bertrand, *Principia Mathematica to *56*,
Cambridge: At the University Press, 1962.

Williams, C. J. F., (1) 'What does "x is true" say about x?' in *Analysis*,
vol. 29, no. 4, 1969.

(2) 'Truth: a Composite Rejoinder' in *Analysis*, vol. 32, no. 2, 1971.

(3) 'Truth: or Bristol Revisited' in *Proceedings of the Aristotelian Society*,
supplementary vol. 47, 1973.

(4) 'Prior on Ontology' in *Ratio*, vol. 15, 1973.

(5) 'Predicating Truth' in *Mind*, vol. 84, 1975.

Index

Williams, Christopher John Fards.
What is truth? / C. J. F. Williams. — Cambridge, Eng. : New York : Cambridge University Press, c1976.

xvi, 102 p. ; 23 cm.

Bibliography: p. 99-101.
Includes index.
ISBN 0-521-20967-6